Get what you
want at work

ROS JAY

Get what you want at work

The complete personal skills guide for career advantage

PEARSON
Prentice Hall
BUSINESS

London • New York • Toronto • Sydney • Tokyo • Singapore • Hong Kong
Cape Town • New Delhi • Madrid • Paris • Amsterdam • Munich • Milan

PEARSON EDUCATION LIMITED

Head Office:
Edinburgh Gate
Harlow CM20 2JE
Tel: +44 (0)1279 623623
Fax: +44 (0)1279 431059

London Office:
128 Long Acre
London WC2E 9AN
Tel: +44 (0)20 7447 2000
Fax: +44 (0)20 7447 2170
Website: www.business-minds.com

First published in Great Britain in 2003

ISBN 0 273 66300 3

British Library Cataloguing in Publication Data
A CIP catalogue record for this book can be obtained from the British Library

Typeset by Northern Phototypesetting Co. Ltd, Bolton
Printed and bound in Great Britain by Bell & Bain Ltd, Glasgow

The Publishers' policy is to use paper manufactured from sustainable forests.

About the author

Ros Jay is a freelance writer and a senior associate of the Institute of Direct Marketing. She specializes in marketing, communications and management-related subjects. She writes and edits corporate magazines both in print and online.

Ros has written many books, including the bestselling *Fast Thinking Managers Manual*, *How to Manage Your Boss*, *How to Get a Pay Rise*, *Brilliant Interview*, *How to Build a Great Team* and *How to Handle Tough Situations at Work*. All are published by Prentice Hall Business.

Contents

So, what do you want?

We all have lists of wants at work. Maybe you want a promotion. Maybe you want to clinch a prestigious deal. Or maybe you just want to get on better with the person at the next desk. Very probably you want lots of things, related to:

- practical reward (such as a pay rise, promotion, or extra perks); or
- job satisfaction (such as making sales, getting a proposal accepted, or improving a system); or
- making your working life easier (such as better relationships, more up-to-date equipment, or more convenient working hours).

Have you noticed how some people seem to get pretty much everything on their list of wants without seeming to put in much effort, while others try hard but get far less for their pains? That's because you need the right set of skills to get what you want. And since your list of wants may vary widely, the set of skills you need is broad too.

You need the right set of skills to get what you want.

Like most people, you're probably very good at getting certain things. You might have working relationships that are the envy of your colleagues, or maybe you're travelling fast up the career ladder, or perhaps you're able to sell anything to anybody. But we all have gaps in our skills. And that's where this book comes in. Here you'll find all the skills you need to get what you want – whether it's for practical reward, job satisfaction, or simply making your life easier.

Once you've learnt and practised these skills, and incorporated them into your normal working life, you'll find that you get what you want most of the time. That will be fine for all those everyday wants, but when something important comes along, you need to be a little more focused in how you use these skills.

Set your objective

Start by setting yourself a clear objective. Don't just tell yourself, for example, 'I want to be better rewarded for my job.' Be precise about what reward you want. A smarter office? A better job title? A pay rise? How much? You can't focus on your target until you can see clearly what it is.

Is it realistic?

Once you have an objective, consider whether it is realistic. There's no point just wanting a pay rise if you don't deserve it. So can you justify it? Or will you be able to justify it in six months' time? Equally, it's no good wanting to tie up a half-million-pound deal with a customer who's never spent more than £50,000 with the company before. Make sure you only put realistic wants on your list; or find a way to make them realistic before you expect to get them.

Plan a strategy

Think through how you'll achieve the objective. What do you need to do? Who do you need to talk to? For example, you might admit if you're honest that you can't really justify a pay rise now, but you will if you can increase your sales over the next six months. So how will you do that? Suppose you are keen to improve your working relationship with a colleague. Should you talk to them? Could you help by adapting your own behaviour? In other words, how are you going to get from where you are now to where you want to be?

Stay focused

Once you know what you're doing, focus on using the skills described in the following chapters to succeed. Follow your plan, monitor your progress and make sure you arrive at your goal. Take other people along with you (you'll find out how in Chapter 3), so that you make friends rather than alienate people along the way. You'll never get what you want if you're not popular.

You'll never get what you want if you're not popular.

By combining the skills you're about to learn with the focus to identify where you're going and how you're going to get there, you'll have everything you need to get what you want at work. Every time.

CHAPTER ONE

Have confidence

Confidence is a huge component of success. You don't have to be big and brash – quiet confidence can be equally impressive. If you don't appear to have confidence in yourself, other people won't have confidence in you either. After all, you should know what you're doing, so they'll follow your lead. Conversely, you'll have noticed how people always feel happy to rely on the more confident people around them, even when they don't really warrant such confidence. It takes quite a few bad experiences before they realize their confidence is misplaced.

Confidence is a huge component of success.

Greeting people

First impressions, and all that. If you can give people the initial impression that you're confident, you're well on your way to projecting a confident image. And confident people are the ones who get what they want. So learn to meet and greet people with confidence. Here are some ways to do it.

- As you approach someone you feel underconfident about greeting, take a deep breath, hold it for a count of three and blow it out through your mouth. (You can easily do this without anyone noticing.) Repeat it if you need to. Then pull yourself up tall as you walk towards the person.

- Always greet people with a smile, the first time you meet and every time.

- Make eye contact; shy people tend to look down at their feet or their hands. Don't be one of them.

- Be ready with a firm handshake (you can practise it on yourself or your friends). Don't fret about whether to shake their hand or not. It's easy to get trapped in a 'to shake or not to shake' dither, which makes both of you look silly. The solution is simple: if you hold out a firm, confident hand, they'll take it. That's the decision made and you'll look supremely confident, warm and friendly.

- Say hello warmly, without waiting to see whether they speak first.
- If you're meeting someone for the first time, introduce yourself (speaking clearly with no mumbling) unless someone else is introducing you. As you hold out your hand and smile, say something like, 'Hello, I'm Ros. Good to meet you.'
- Use confident body language. This basically means look relaxed – arms by your sides or in your lap if you're sitting – but alert. So make eye contact and look interested. The things to avoid are folding your arms (a very defensive gesture), putting your hands in front of your face, and perching on the edge of your chair if you're sitting down.

Plan ahead

Decide in advance what you'll say and do and then there's no need for dithering – you can say it with confidence. Decide to proffer a hand, to say hello, to smile, to introduce yourself. The more often you do each of these things, the more of a habit it becomes, so that soon you'll do it automatically. Then you'll look truly cool and confident.

Sounding confident

When it comes to speaking, you want to reinforce your confident image. So here are a few pointers.

- Speak clearly, without mumbling, and don't talk so softly that people have to strain to hear you.
- Decide in advance what words you will use to say something, so you can say it with confidence when the time comes.
- Role play nerve-wracking conversations in advance with a friend or in front of a mirror.
- When you talk to someone, if you start to feel nervous about how you're coming across, give yourself a quick talking to. You should be concen-

trating on them – being interested in what they're saying. Stop thinking about you and focus on them. Not only is it a more generous approach, but it will also stop you worrying and make you appear far more confident.

If you cast doubt on your own abilities, others will doubt you too. So if you're asked to give your first presentation or meet an important customer, don't say, 'Ooh, I don't know if I can handle it. I'm not very good at that sort of thing. I'm worried I'll let you down.' You don't have to pretend to be totally cool, but don't undermine others' confidence in you. Say something like, 'I've never done it before, but I'm sure I can. So long as I get plenty of support, it'll be fine. And I'll enjoy the challenge.'

> **Role play nerve-wracking conversations in advance with a friend or in front of a mirror.**

Creating real confidence

If you are – or feel you are – particularly shy or nervous, bear in mind that the better you know what you're doing, the more confident you will be. If you are nervous when meeting people, plan in advance what you will say. Practise in front of a mirror, if you like. Decide whether you will proffer a hand to shake immediately or wait for them to do so first. Be ready and prepared and you'll have nothing to feel shy or nervous about.

The same goes for scary experiences like delivering reports, giving presentations, running meetings and so on. Plan what you're going to do, go on courses or read up on the subject, and give yourself plenty of preparation time. With speeches, presentations and so on, rehearse over and over until you know exactly what you're doing. It does more for confidence than anything else.

> **Confidence is largely a matter of practice. Go through the motions a few times and it will start to become habit.**

Summary

Confidence is largely a matter of practice. Go through the motions a few times and it will start to become habit. Before you know it, you really will feel more confident than before. You simply need to:

Greet people confidently

- Smile.
- Make eye contact.
- Offer a firm handshake.
- Say hello.
- Use confident body language.

Sound confident

- Speak clearly.
- Rehearse what you're going to say.
- Focus on the other person and don't worry about how you're coming across.

Practise until you really are confident

- Prepare what you're going to say.
- Rehearse with a friend or in front of a mirror.

CHAPTER TWO

Be assertive

You'll never get what you want at work unless you can be assertive. Assertiveness is a skill which very few of us are born with. We have to learn how to do it and, while many of us can do it some of the time, few of us can do it all of the time without practice. So what is it? Before answering that question, let's just see whether you recognize either of these scenarios.

You'll never get what you want at work unless you can be assertive.

Scenario 1

Your boss calls you in, looking very displeased. They've just been told by one of their fellow managers that you turned up half an hour late for a vital interdepartmental meeting yesterday. They are extremely disappointed – you've let the whole team down. You start to explain but they tell you there's no excuse for such behaviour. You mumble an apology and get out as fast as you can.

OK, so that's not you. Let's try this version.

Scenario 2

Your boss calls you in, looking very displeased. They've just been told by one of their fellow managers that you turned up half an hour late for a vital interdepartmental meeting yesterday. They are extremely disappointed – you've let the whole team down. When you hear this,

---

you're furious – it wasn't your fault. The manager in question changed the time and the message never reached you. You lay into your boss, complaining about the other manager, and the fact that your boss thinks you would do such a thing without a valid reason. Then you storm out.

If you're wondering which of these is supposed to be the assertive version, the answer is neither of them (OK, so you probably guessed that). In fact, assertiveness is the form of behaviour that prevents either of these scenarios from happening. So before we look in detail at how to be assertive, let's look at the alternatives to assertiveness, and why we don't want to use them. Assertiveness is a balanced approach between two extremes. If assertiveness is the fulcrum in the centre of the see-saw, the two opposite extremes are submission and aggression.

Submission

The first scenario is classic submissive behaviour. Rather than risk confrontation, we succumb to the temptation to take the easy route. Don't answer back, don't stand up to the boss in case it puts their back up. Submissive behaviour always means taking what appears to be the easy route, so it includes:

- Keeping your feelings hidden.
- Saying what you think the other person wants to hear.
- Apologizing even when it's not your fault.
- Taking on more work rather than saying 'no'.
- Allowing people to take advantage of you.

Our submissive behaviour may work for everybody around us, but it doesn't work so well for us.

Recognize any of these? Many of us are submissive at least some of the time, at least with certain people (the boss is often one of them). In the short term it avoids unpleasantness and conflict. So what's wrong with it?

Our submissive behaviour may work for everybody around us, but it doesn't work so well for us. Here are just a few examples of the damage it can do.

- Bottling up feelings can lead to dissatisfaction, demotivation and general work stress.

- For some people, hiding their feelings only lasts so long. Then they explode in a display of aggression, which has its own disadvantages (as we'll see in a moment).

- Suppressing our feelings can also lead to resentment and ill-feeling towards the person we are submissive towards.

- If we never disagree openly with people, many of our best ideas never get aired. As well as being extremely frustrating, this means we're not making the contribution we should.

- Keeping your head down also makes it very hard for you to take the kind of risks or promote the controversial ideas that can earn you respect, reward and promotion.

> **If we never disagree openly with people, many of our best ideas never get aired.**

- Apologizing when it's not your fault will give people the impression that you *are* to blame.

- We can end up overworked through being unable to say 'no', and through allowing others to take advantage of our excessively good nature.

That should give you some idea why submissive behaviour isn't a good thing. It can lead to stress, demotivation, resentment, overwork, professional frustration, missing out on promotion and pay rises . . . to name but a few of the points against it.

Aggression

So what about the other end of the scale? Some of us behave aggressively because we feel it gets us what we want. Some of us even do it when the pressure valve finally blows after all that submissive behaviour. So what is it that we think will get us what we want?

- Telling people exactly what we think rather than bottling up feelings – even when it is hurtful or offensive.

- Pushing our own ideas forward, at the expense of others' ideas if necessary.

- Telling people where to get off if they try to take advantage of us.

- Intimidating other people by raising our voices or using offensive or threatening language.

It's quite true that aggressive behaviour can often get you what you want – in the short term. And some of us aren't really *very* aggressive, after all; we're just a bit aggressive occasionally. That's OK, isn't it?

Well no, not really. Even displaying only occasional aggressive behaviour means that others are permanently aware of the threat of aggression from us. Occasional moderate aggression may not be as bad as frequent strong aggression, but it's still a bad thing.

Alright then, what's so wrong with using a technique that gets us what we want? Here's an idea of some of the problems an aggressive manner can bring you.

- People often won't tell us things because of the risk of an aggressive response. For example, our colleagues may not tell us how our working relationship with them could be improved; or our boss might not let us know what was wrong with the report we submitted (so how will we be able to improve on it next time and earn more credit?).

- We will get an unpleasant reputation among our colleagues, subordinates, boss and other managers, which will do nothing for our prospects of being given interesting and stimulating tasks, especially if they involve co-operating with others. And it will do nothing for our chances of promotion either.

- If we're pushy about our own ideas, other people's resentment may tempt them to reject our ideas for personal reasons, regardless of their merit.

- If we are offensive or hurtful to others, they are more likely to be offensive or hurtful to us.

- Adopting an intimidating or unpleasant tone when dealing with others means we will far more frequently find ourselves in arguments and conflicts, which are not the most effective way of resolving differences, since everyone tends to dig their heels in.

If we are offensive or hurtful to others, they are more likely to be offensive or hurtful to us.

There. We'll get a bad reputation, we won't be told things we need to hear, our ideas are less likely to be adopted, people will treat us unpleasantly, we'll end up in more arguments and conflicts, and we'll damage our chances of promotion. That's not an exhaustive list, but it should be enough to persuade you that aggression is no smarter a tactic in the long run than submissiveness. So that just leaves us with the mid-point where the two behaviours balance out: assertiveness.

Assertiveness

Assertive behaviour carries all the advantages of both these extremes, without the disadvantages. It is an easy route to take, and it gets us what we want. What's more, it works in the long term as well as the short term. Once you've learnt the basic techniques, you can be assertive all of the time instead of just some of the time, and you'll start to appreciate the benefits. Here are some of them.

Assertive behaviour is an easy route to take, and it gets us what we want.

- You'll be able to express how you feel, without confrontation, so there'll be no more bottled-up feelings, frustrations and the stress that goes with them.
- Others will be able to respond to your feelings in a calm and measured manner, so that you'll feel your voice is heard.
- Other people will be able to express their views and feelings to you, so you can rely on being told the things you need to hear.
- You'll learn to put forward even controversial ideas without conflict, so you can air all your views and feel more involved. People will be happy to accept your ideas if they agree with them.
- This means you'll be able to take credit for your own ideas.
- You'll earn a reputation for being easy to work with, so people will want you on the team for interesting and prestigious projects.
- You will earn the respect of your boss, your colleagues and your team.
- People will treat you with the respect that you give them, making your working relationships pleasant.
- You won't ever again find yourself overworked simply through being unable to say 'no'.

That's a pretty persuasive list of reasons why it's worth learning to be more assertive. Whichever end of the scale you tend to veer towards – submission or aggression, or even a mix of the two – assertiveness has got to be a better way. And it's not difficult. The only thing that takes practice is learning to suppress your habitual response, whether it's submissive or aggressive, and replace it with the assertive approach. Before long, assertiveness will become the habit, and you won't even have to think about it any more.

So how do you do this assertiveness thing? Well, there are five key skills you have to master. You probably use all of these at times, and some of them may already be easy for you. It's just a matter of incorporating them all into your mainstream approach, rather than keeping them as an occasional add-on:

1 Show respect for others.

2 Express your feelings.

3 Be honest.

4 Learn to stand your ground.

5 Be able to say 'no'.

Let's look at each of these in turn.

Show respect for others

Here's one for the naturally aggressive among us. It's an important factor, whatever your natural inclinations, but people with aggressive tendencies usually find it the hardest to master.

If we are going to expect respect and fair treatment from others we must give as good as we want to get.

A large part of the principle of assertiveness is about respect, but it has to work both ways. If we are going to expect respect and fair treatment from others – which we will if we are assertive – we must give as good as we want to get. So showing respect for others is all about demonstrating the behaviour we want to receive back. We need to:

- allow other people to have opinions without shouting them down or criticizing them unfairly;
- listen carefully when others are speaking (that's what Chapter 6 is all about);

- choose friendly and constructive ways of making negative comments;
- speak calmly and fairly when we disagree with someone, without raising our voices, or becoming offensive or personal;
- give encouragement to other people, and praise them when they do well.

These are all behaviours we'd like to be on the receiving end of, so we should demonstrate them to other people. And being assertive means behaving like this with everyone, not just a select few people whom we deal with frequently, or whom we think are useful to us.

Impress your boss

If you're inclined towards aggression, just think how this new, assertive you could transform your relationship with your boss. They will change their view of you, and come to see you as a mature, pleasant person with whom everyone – including them – is happy to work.

Express your feelings

This one's for both the submissive and the aggressive. Submissive people need to learn to say what they feel, while the aggressive need to learn *how* to say it in a more assertive manner. As an assertive person, you recognize your right to express your feelings and have them heard; you also recognize the right of others to be told your feelings in a way that won't upset them.

If someone makes you feel angry, hurt, offended, sidelined, humiliated or anything else, the assertive response is to tell them so. After all, if you don't tell them, how will they know? You deserve to have your feelings considered, but they don't have the option of doing this if you don't tell them how you feel.

There are several ways to tell someone how you feel. You could start by saying, for example:

1 You're making me angry by . . .

2 I don't like you saying . . . because . . .

3 I feel . . . when you . . .

4 You're being offensive . . .

Only one of these options is assertive; that is to say it expresses how you feel without provoking a confrontational response. (I'll tell you which one in a moment.) The other person may not even realize the effect they're having on you, so if you show respect you won't want to upset them by being aggressive. If they *are* aware of the response they generate in you, you still don't want a confrontation. Apart from the unpleasantness of it, it's not likely to resolve the issue.

So which approach will be assertive, and make your point without causing a row? The answer is the third one. It puts the focus firmly on you and your feelings, rather than on the other person's behaviour, while still making the point. There's no hint of accusation in it; it's merely a statement of fact. For example: 'I feel frustrated when you check up on my work closely. I feel I'm not trusted to do a good job by myself.'

Whenever you want to express your feelings, in a group meeting or one-to-one, use this approach. Focus on yourself and start by saying, 'I feel . . . when . . . ' and take it from there. So long as you continue in the same vein, showing respect for the other person, there's no reason for a confrontation to develop.

Taking them by surprise

Your boss or one of your colleagues may be in the habit of walking all over you. In this case, it may take them by surprise when you start to express how you feel. Or they may be used to you standing up to them, creating rows and being difficult to handle. Either way, they will find you far easier to work with once you adopt an assertive approach.

Be honest

You have a right to be honest. If you like, you can see this as a right to express your negative feelings as well as your positive ones. So if you dis-agree, or you don't want to do something, say so. If you think about this, it's much fairer towards who-ever you're dealing with, too. Otherwise they will probably sense something is amiss but won't know what.

If you're going to be honest, don't beat about the bush – tell it straight.

If you're going to be honest, don't beat about the bush – tell it straight. If you're not happy, say 'I'm not happy.' If you disagree, say 'I disagree.' Don't confuse everyone and under-rate the importance of your feelings by saying, 'Hmm, I'm not sure. I mean, I'm sure it's fine . . . it's just that . . . it's great, but . . . well, you know . . .' Spit it out and you'll achieve two benefits:

1   Everyone will know what your point of view really is.

2   You will have asserted clearly your right to say what you think or feel.

If your natural tendency is towards submissiveness, you will find it hard at first to state your opinions and feelings clearly. However, as soon as you try it you'll find it's really far easier than you think. If you're more prone to aggressive behaviour, you may be tempted to be honest to the point of being blunt, or even rude. This is something you have to watch out for, so pick your words carefully and express your feelings without upsetting or offending anyone.

Express your feelings without upsetting or offending anyone.

This is easiest if you simply avoid emotive or negative words and stick to statements of fact. So instead of saying, 'That's rubbish,' say, 'I don't agree with that.' Instead of saying, 'I think we should scrap your idea,' say, 'I think we should reconsider.'

Mind your language

Assertive people use clear but constructive language, and look for phrases which encourage unity. They also remember that other people's views are as important as their own. So to be assertive you need to use expressions such as:

- I feel . . .
- I'd like to . . .
- Shall we . . .
- How about . . .
- What do you think?
- How do you feel?

Learn to stand your ground

As an assertive person, you should be able to fend off attempts to intimidate you, without becoming defensive and emotional. If a particular person is inclined to bludgeon you, you need to learn how to assert your position without causing trouble. Don't be pressured into changing your opinion or putting up with something you're not happy with. There are two options for handling this kind of situation.

1 State assertively how you feel. 'I'm not happy,' or 'I feel pressured.' This makes the position plain to the other person, and you can then follow the guidelines for expressing your feelings that we looked at earlier.

2 Adopt the 'stuck record' technique. This involves stating your position clearly and then repeating it as often as necessary. Don't become emotional or heated, just stick to your guns. For example, if your boss is trying to give you responsibility you don't feel ready for, say: 'I don't feel ready to take on the scheduling on my own yet.' If they pressure you, repeat it: 'I need more training before I feel ready to take on the scheduling by myself.' Just carry on with this as long as you need to: 'I'm not happy about taking on the scheduling on my own. I need more training.' It's only a matter of time before they get the point.

Look the part

Assertive body language will help to back up your assertive language. If you look nervous and submissive, this will send messages to the other person which contradict your words. The same goes for aggressive, overbearing posture. Assertive body language:

- is upright but relaxed;
- doesn't impinge on the other person's personal space;
- involves plenty of direct eye contact.

Be able to say 'no'

If you are under-assertive, you may well find it difficult to say no to people who ask you favours. There's the worry you might make them angry, or that they will dislike you or be disappointed in you. But in fact, if you think about it, we all know plenty of people who are able to say no without losing popularity or respect, and without causing conflict.

If you avoid saying no, you will find your workload slowly increasing, and you may often take on tasks you're not happy to be doing. Some of us find a middle ground by saying no and lying about the reason, 'I can't do that, I'm afraid, I have an important meeting to go to.' This may get you off the hook, but it generally leaves you feeling uncomfortable, not to say worried that the other person will find out you've lied to them.

So the assertive answer is simply to say no when you want to. And again, this is actually fairer on the person you're dealing with. If they know you'll say no if you want to, they won't feel uncomfortable asking you to do things for them. If you start saying no to people,

The assertive answer is simply to say no when you want to.

you may put yourself through agony the first couple of times trying to pluck up the courage, but once you've said it you usually find the other person thinks it's no big deal. 'OK. Fair enough,' they reply, and cheerfully wander off to find another solution.

Here are a few tips for saying no.

- Remind yourself that you are quite entitled to say no, and there is no reason to feel guilty.

- It may help you feel better to give a brief explanation of why you're saying no. You don't have to do this, but it can feel more co-operative. So rather than say, 'I don't have time to do that', you may feel happier saying, 'I don't have time to do that – I'm already covering for Sandy this week'.

- You may also feel more helpful if you offer a different solution to their problem. For example, 'I don't have time to find the answer for you, but I can tell you where to find it yourself', or, 'I can't do it for you now, but if you can wait until Monday I'll be able to do it then'.

- If the other person is persistent, use the stuck record technique. Suppose your boss wants you to stay late; there's nothing in your contract that says you have to and on this occasion it would be really inconvenient, too. Just keep saying no until they get the message: 'I'm afraid I can't work late on Friday.' If they reiterate the request, reply, 'I'm sorry, but I can't work late on Friday. I have to take my mother to the hospital.' (You're not obliged to give a reason, but if you're happy to, it often helps.) If they ask again, just keep telling them, 'I'm sorry, I can't do Friday.' Don't raise your voice or get upset; just be clear and assertive.

Practice makes perfect

If you have a repeated situation where you find it hard to be assertive, think through the assertive response and then rehearse it until you feel ready to put it into practice. Perhaps a particular colleague per-sistently puts you down in meetings. Decide how you will handle it and run through the words until you feel comfortable with them. You could get another colleague or someone at home to role play it with you.

It's not easy to change personality overnight. If you're usually assertive, these guidelines will help you to become assertive even more of the time. If, however, you are more often either submissive or aggressive, it will take you a little while to perfect the new, assertive you. And it will also take a while for people to notice the change. So don't expect other people's attitude towards you to change instantly. But give it time, keep being assertive, and before long people will stop trying to walk all over you once they learn it doesn't work, or will stop being defensive once they realize you are no longer aggressive.

Summary

Assertiveness means being neither submissive nor aggressive. You need to:

- Show respect for other people.
- Express your feelings.
- Be honest.
- Learn to stand your ground.
- Be able to say 'no'.

CHAPTER THREE

Manage people

Getting what you want often requires other people's co-operation, especially when you're working on a project that means a lot to you. Perhaps it's one that will get you noticed for promotion, or will make your job more rewarding. When you need other people to help you, you have to handle them the right way so that they not only give you the help you want, but give it willingly. That way, no one feels exploited or bears grudges. And, of course, there are often times when someone has no obligation to do what you ask, and simply won't help you unless they feel motivated to do so.

Getting what you want often requires other people's co-operation.

So whether your help is coming from people who've been told to help you or from people who are doing you favours, you still need to motivate them to do their best. It's down to you to make sure that they say yes to helping out, and that they really put everything they've got into it. So this chapter is all about the techniques you can use to make sure you get all the support you need from other people, whether it's one colleague helping for ten minutes or a whole team giving up several days to something you want to be a big success.

Motivation

The key to the whole thing is motivation. If other people want to help, you're laughing. The question is, how can you motivate them? The first thing you need to appreciate is that in other people's eyes, working for you and working for whatever project you need help with amounts to much the same thing; you are the project. However much they care about the work being successful, they must also want to do the best they can for you in order to feel fully motivated.

Clearing time

Part of what demotivates people is being asked or expected to do work they just haven't got time for. The stress of fitting everything into the day makes them resentful. So always give people as much notice as you can that you'll need their help, even if you can't tell them exactly what you'll need until nearer the time. That way, at least they can free up the time for you.

Suppose you're trying to organize the best ever Christmas party – everyone will have fun and you'll be remembered and appreciated for it. Your team of helpers might want the office party to go with a swing, but if you demoralize or upset them, they won't do their best. Even if they work hard, they'll work hard at the bits they're interested in, which may not be what you want them to work at. They'll all be happy to blow up balloons, but no one will want to count out 300 napkins and arrange them in alternating colours to suit your scheme.

> **Always give people as much notice as you can that you'll need their help.**

Clearly this is even more important if the project *doesn't* motivate the people working with you. Perhaps it doesn't matter in the least to your colleague in another department whether you get this particular newsletter to the printers on time. Maybe your receptionist is dead against the idea of an open day. But you've still got to persuade them that they want to put a real effort into it. They'll only be doing it for you. If they don't care about you either, you're sunk.

What's in it for them?

People are motivated by the prospect of reward. And different rewards suit different people. So the question you need to ask yourself of each individual helper is, 'What's in it for them?' The answer won't be the same for each person.

There's a limit to what you can offer them, too. You're presumably not in a position to offer a company car or an extra two weeks' annual holiday, or even a salary rise. But that's OK. You're not asking them to sacrifice their marriage or risk serious personal injury. You're only asking them for a few hours of their time, so the reward can be more modest.

People are motivated by the prospect of reward. And different rewards suit different people.

There are two types of reward you can give people. There are the rewards you can flag up in advance ('If you help me out this evening, I'll give you the afternoon off on Friday'), and there are rewards which you don't necessarily promise in advance but which experience should soon teach people that they'll get from you (such as writing an official note to their department head about how tremendously helpful they were).

Time teaches

Every time you run a project, you should be generous in your appreciation in ways which mean something to the person concerned. They will soon learn to trust that you will reward them, even if you don't spell out the reward in advance.

So what you need now are ideas for the kind of rewards you can give to people who help you achieve what you want. People should still be rewarded, whether they are doing you a favour or whether they haven't been given a choice about helping you. Here are some of the typical motivating factors you can use to encourage people to put real effort into this thing.

Money

Here's one of the most obvious motivators. You may not always be able to use it but often you can, especially if you're using your own team members to help. If you expect them to work extra hours, it's quite reasonable to let them know that this will be reflected in their Christmas bonus, or taken into account at their next salary review.

Status

Some people don't care two hoots about this, but others get a big kick out of it. For people who want status, give them the job of dealing with senior management, or interviewing your top customer for the company news-letter. Or tell them that since the valuable demonstration model has to be loaded into their car, you've cleared it for them to park in the MD's parking space since it's nearest the entrance. Or ask them to carry out a particular task with their own team of helpers.

Recognition

This is different from appreciation (which we'll come to in a moment) because it involves broadcasting their achievements to other people. Whether or not you tell them you'll do this, you can recognize people's efforts for many kinds of help with an article or thank-you in the company newsletter, or by writing to their head of department, or even the MD, to say how pleased you were with their help.

Responsibility

Some people are itching to prove – to themselves or to you – that they can handle responsibility. So put them in charge of organizing an event for you, or give them responsibility for the layout and presentation of the major report you're trying to get finished. These people may well get a big kick out of being given a team of assistants to help them.

Job satisfaction

For many people, knowing they have done the job well is a big part of their reward, even before you've noticed it and thanked them. Give these people a complete job to look after, from start to finish, that they can take pride in. It might be organizing the car parking, decorating the venue for the party or putting together all your disparate notes into a smart and informative press pack.

Challenge

This is often related to job satisfaction, but it involves stretching people – giving them something to do that is difficult, or which they've never done before. Ask these people to get the demonstration model working, or to handle all the contact with outside suppliers.

Appreciation

Just about everyone will want to know that you appreciate the fact that they are working extra hours for you, or that they have had to delay their other work to fit this in. So notice good work and thank people for it. Not just at the end of the project, but throughout. As you rush past the recently laid out buffet table it doesn't hurt to say, 'That looks nice.' When someone hands you a neatly typed contents

Notice good work and thank people for it.

page and summary for the report, you can say, 'Thanks – that was quick!' Always be ready to show appreciation; it's what makes people feel it was worth putting in the effort for you.

Specific thanks

A quick thanks in passing is fine, but when someone completes a task, give them more detailed thanks to show you're sincere and genuinely appreciative. So always aim to comment on a particular aspect of the task that they've done well: 'That was fast!', or 'I like the way you've allowed plenty of space in the layout so it looks really readable', or 'That's a good idea – I'd never have thought of setting the chairs out that way round, but it works much better like that.'

Clearly you can combine two or more of these motivating factors for most people. In any case, you should always show appreciation. That may be plenty for someone who's given you five minutes of their time, but for people who are putting in a few hours or even a couple of days, give them a little more to keep them motivated.

Before you allocate tasks to your team members and volunteers, think about which tasks will motivate each person. It may be that no one is going to find the job of sweeping the floor of the venue very inspiring, but someone will do a good job of it for enough reward – and thanks from you may be sufficient.

Creating an atmosphere

Everybody works better when they're enjoying themselves. So make this fun, especially if you're working on a big, high profile project. Your aim should be that anyone who isn't involved in this project of yours will feel

Everybody works better when they're enjoying themselves. So make this fun.

they've missed out. So put on your best sense of humour, and create a party atmosphere if you can – or failing that, a blitz mentality – in order to generate a sense of team spirit and shared objectives. Send out for cream cakes for everyone, have a competition to see who can set out their row of chairs fastest (without sacrificing neatness), offer a bottle of wine to the first person who completes their newsletter article.

If there are any boring tasks going, put people in pairs or threes to do them. Give three people three tasks to do together instead of dishing out one job each. They'll have more fun that way. Putting people together to do groups of jobs is how Volvo build cars.

This is easiest to do when everyone is working in the same geographical area, but even with, say, newsletter contributors sending in material from different offices, you can still generate enthusiasm with humorous but genuine e-mail updates to everyone. Yes, it takes a few moments, but if it speeds everyone else up, it's worth it.

Don't do too much

If you are lucky enough to have several people to help you, don't even attempt to get any of the tasks done yourself. You won't be able to, and you'll end up achieving less rather than more. With several assistants, your job is solely to co-ordinate everyone else, check completed tasks, brief on fresh tasks and distribute thanks and praise. That's more important than anything else. You can combine it with a mundane task that you don't mind being called away from frequently – such as setting out the glasses, plates and cutlery – but don't try to do anything demanding.

Your own attitude

It's vital that you should be popular – even under stress. These people are working hard to keep you happy. So make sure they want you to be happy.

If they make mistakes, be generous. Otherwise they'll do it on purpose next time. Don't be too bossy, and always ask people to do tasks rather than telling them (even if they are obliged to do what you tell them).

> **Don't be too bossy, and always ask people to do tasks rather than telling them.**

And however stressed and frustrated you get, don't take it out on your workers. They're doing their best, and if you add to their stress, their work will deteriorate. If necessary, hide in a cupboard and scream or punch the walls until you feel better.

> **Muck in**
>
> You will make yourself far more popular if you muck in and do the boring or unpleasant jobs along with everyone else. If they see you cleaning or pinning up notices, they can hardly complain if you ask them to do something equally mundane. And your popularity rating will shoot up. The key to good management is popularity.

Striking the right tone

If you're trying to persuade people to do something for nothing (or to do a lot for not very much), you may need to put some effort into how you ask. Some people will naturally be very co-operative, but others may resist helping and you need to think through how you're going to ask them for help or favours in advance. Whether it's a supplier, a colleague, your boss or the head of another department, the key is to decide what you're going to say before you speak to them.

It's no good pretending to be someone you're not – it will simply sound false – but most of us have a range of personas we can draw on. You might feel quite comfortable saying, 'Listen, mate, any chance of a favour?' to one person, and, 'I'm so sorry to bother you, but I wonder if you could possibly help me out?' to the next. So think about the best words to use to suit the person you're dealing with. This applies to the actual favour, too. Should you give them the background first, or just come straight out with it?

Think about the best words to use to suit the person you're dealing with.

Should you try to make it sound like less work than you suspect it really will be, or should you tell it like it is?

And it's not only the words – it's the tone, too. Some people respond well to cajoling, others just get wound up by it. Some people don't want to be told they owe you a favour even if they do – it feels like emotional blackmail – while others are happy to have it pointed out. This isn't as complicated as it sounds – the point is that many people just don't think these things through in advance, but you'll have more success if you do.

Fair's fair

You're asking people for favours here; that means they're entitled to say no. And for all you know, they may have good reason to. You don't want to say yes to every favour *you're* asked, after all. So be gracious when you're refused. Don't sulk, or you can bet that the person concerned will never want to say yes to you in future. If you're magnanimous, on the other hand ('Fair enough – I can see you're really busy'), they are much more likely to feel guilty and say yes next time.

Make sure your body language isn't overbearing or aggressive, either. Don't hold constant eye contact, lean too close to the person or use any dominant gestures such as finger-wagging or table-thumping. All these types of body language give the impression you're trying to intimidate the other person into saying yes. It will work with submissive people (although they will do the work reluctantly rather than enthusiastically), but it will have the opposite effect with stronger personalities.

If this all sounds horribly complicated to remember, it really isn't. Don't worry. If you're not feeling intimidating or aggressive you won't appear as if you are. So convince yourself you're asking for a favour which the other person has every right to refuse, and you should find that the tone and the body language take care of themselves.

Relationships and networks

The more people you have strong relationships with, the better chance you have of getting what you want. Other people have it in their power to give or withhold favours, resources and co-operation. The more people you know, and the better terms you're on with them, the more chance you have that they will give you what you need.

Getting to know people

The more people you know the better. It stands to reason. If you need co-operation from another department, for example, you've a better chance if you know someone in that department than if you don't. Or perhaps you want advice from someone with financial experience. If you know one of the senior accountants, you can pick their brains. Or maybe you want to apply for an internal job that's come up. It'll be a big help if the person interviewing the candidates already knows you.

If you know one of the senior accountants, you can pick their brains.

So how do you get to know people? For a start it helps to be confident and friendly, and willing to talk to new people when you encounter them. On top of that, here are a few more ways to build a network of useful contacts.

- Get involved in cross-departmental projects. Whether it's editing the internal newsletter, organizing the Christmas party or running the exhibition stand at the NEC, anything that brings you into contact with other people in the organization will help.

- Turn up to any social get-togethers you can where you'll get to know people better. This doesn't mean you have to give up your private life; it just means that if everyone else is going for lunch together, or out for a drink after work, go along too. You don't have to go out with your own team every time, but go along if there are new people there.

- Don't be afraid to make an initial contact with someone. If you want advice from an accountant, for example, just contact them cold. Once you've made that initial move, you'll know them for next time you speak to them, and you've added them to your network.

- If you don't know the person you need, find someone else to put you in touch. They can speak to the person for you, or you could just use their name (but always check first).

Spread your net

Don't limit yourself to people inside your organization. Make and maintain contacts with people outside, too, including customers, suppliers, people who have left your organization to work elsewhere, useful contacts you make through personal friends, people you used to work with in other companies, and so on.

Building relationships

Once you've got to know these people, you need to build and maintain strong relationships with them all.

- Keep in touch with these people once you know them: have a quick chat in the car park when you pass them, or get in touch to talk to them about other projects. You might call and offer them equipment your department no longer needs, or information you think they might find useful. Or you can call them to ask a favour or pick their brains. Just keep in touch or the relationship will peter out.

- Send them Christmas cards, invite them to events and functions and generally find as many opportunities as you can to remind them of the relationship.

- Do your best to give these people as much as they give you. If you're always calling on them to help out, the relationship can sour if they begin to see you as a bit of a pest. So redress the balance whenever you can. Do your very best to co-operate whenever they want something from you, and don't always wait to be asked. If you can see a way to help them, do it.

- There are some people, often those senior to you, who simply don't need as much from you as you need from them. Don't pester them, but one thing that you can do is to pick their brains. So long as you don't keep taking up valuable time, people are flattered that you want their advice and therefore will usually give it willingly.

So long as you don't keep taking up valuable time, people are flattered that you want their advice and therefore will usually give it willingly.

By building up a network of good relationships with people inside and outside the organization, you will have a great resource to call on to help you get what you want at work. And the best part of it is when you find that you, in return, can help them to get what *they* want too.

Summary

In order to get the best out of the people you work with, remember the following:

- Motivate them to help you.
- Show them what's in it for them.
- Create a stimulating atmosphere.
- Be positive and appreciative, even if you're feeling stressed.
- Build strong relationships and networks.

CHAPTER FOUR

Deal with difficult behaviour

There are times when getting on with other people is a doddle. Everything's going well, you know what you're doing and you can do it well. And then there are the other times. When you're under stress – or someone else is – there's a tendency to get emotional. You may be winding each other up, or outside factors may be making one or both of you stressed. Either way, you can end up taking it out on each other if you're not careful.

> **Heightened emotions can get in the way of a good working relationship with anyone.**

Heightened emotions, unless they are positive ones, get in the way of a good working relationship with anyone – your colleagues, your subordinates or your boss. So you need to be able to control your own emotions, and you also need to be able to handle their emotions so that you can calm them down rather than inflame them.

Your emotions

The first step to handling unconstructive emotion in other people is to stay calm, so it stands to reason that the first skill to master is controlling your own emotions. With many people this is rarely a problem, but with some it can certainly be a challenge. Whether they make you feel angry, irritable, tearful or anything else, you need to find a way to keep on top of your response.

I'm not suggesting that your response may not be entirely justified. But showing your emotions is never going to be the quickest or the most effective way to resolve things in the short term, nor the best step towards a good relationship in the long term. What's more, to the kind of person who provokes this response, your display of feeling can come across as emotional blackmail. It may appear to say, 'Look what you've done! You made me cry / get angry / get irritable . . . ' As soon as emotional blackmail – real or imagined – enters the equation, you're in trouble. That starts to look like game-playing and manipulation, and you don't want to be a part of that, since it makes a strong relationship with other people impossible. A good relationship must be based on honesty and trust. (We'll look at how to handle other people's emotional blackmail later on.)

A good relationship must be based on honesty and trust.

All this doesn't mean you should bottle up your emotions. As we saw in Chapter 2, you should certainly express how you feel. But you need to express yourself calmly in words, not by emotional demonstration. And to do that, you have to be able to stay calm. Once you're calm, you can choose your words carefully to make sure that what you say is constructive rather than confrontational.

Separate home and work

Although you should aim to present as calm a front as you can at work, and not be given to bouts of rage, sulking or tears, there is an exception. You are allowed to be tearful about non-work related upsets. This should hopefully happen rarely if ever, but if you've just taken a phone call telling you about a family bereavement, for example, you're not expected to bite your tongue and show no response. You're allowed to be human.

Some of us find staying calm easier than others. If you find it tough, here are a few ideas to help you.

- Focus on your objective, which is to resolve the conflict that is generating these feelings. Recognize that staying calm will help you achieve this faster and more effectively.

- Use feedback (we'll look at this later in the chapter) to resolve things without emotional displays.

- If someone's behaviour makes you feel tearful or angry, don't listen to it. Once you've got the point, they are probably repeating themselves anyway if they're angry. So look them in the eye and count to 20, or think about something that makes you happy. In any case, you're not going to be able to resolve things until they're also calm and reasonable.

- If they are emotional, use the techniques described later in this chapter to calm them down.

- If you feel unable to restrain your emotions, just leave. If you need to give a reason, just be honest: 'I'm feeling too emotional to discuss this now. I'm going to leave, and I'll discuss it with you when I feel calmer.'

Other people's emotions

Once you've learnt to control your own emotions, you can start to handle other people's emotions, too, from a position of strength. Now you're calm and rational, you are in a far better position to get *them* back on track. Probably the most common negative emotion you're likely to encounter is anger, so we'll look at how to handle that first.

There are two types of anger you might encounter: justified anger and unjustified or tactical anger. You need to handle these two emotions in very different ways.

Justified anger

The best adjusted people don't make emotional displays of anger, no matter how out of line you are. They express their feelings through words, not actions. But there are times when people do have cause to be angry with others.

> **The best adjusted people don't make emotional displays of anger, no matter how out of line you are.**

Let the punishment fit the crime

For anger to be justified it must be in proportion to the offence. If, for example, your boss spends three hours screaming at you for being two minutes late for the first time in a year, that's not justified anger. But if they spend ten minutes sounding off at you for a stupid mistake that has cost the organization £20,000 in sales, that's justified (even if it would have been better to handle it without raising their voice).

So what do you do when your boss – or even a colleague – gives you a legitimate dressing down? If you're out of line, the answer is that you:

- admit it
- apologize
- offer to make reparation, if it's possible.

It's as simple as that.

There is another category of justified anger, however, which you are far more likely to encounter (since I'm sure you would never make stupid mistakes, such as the example above). Someone may be understandably angry about something which is actually a misunderstanding, or which you could not have foreseen the result of. Suppose a colleague in another department has just got into trouble with *their* boss because their budget is late – the reason being that you still haven't submitted the figures they need from you. No wonder they're angry. In fact, however, you've been badly let down by a supplier who kept promising you the figures you needed but never came up with them despite you chasing them frequently.

The result is that your colleague is very angry at being let down. How do you handle the situation and defuse their anger? For a start, you stay calm, as we've already seen. But then what?

- People who get angry for a legitimate reason tend to do so because they feel they won't get the response they want otherwise. They fear they won't be listened to or taken seriously. Your colleague is worried that if they don't get angry with you, you won't learn for next time the importance of getting the figures to them on time. So the first thing to do is to listen fully to them (follow the guidelines in Chapter 6) so they can see you're taking in what they're saying.

- Now show them you feel their anger is justified. Not necessarily that directing it at you is justified, but that anger is an understandable response. Legitimize their feelings by sympathizing with them (without apologizing if it's not your fault): 'I can see why you're feeling angry,' or, 'You must be incredibly frustrated.'

- Don't spend ages justifying your actions. It will just sound as if you're making excuses. They're angry about their own problems; they don't want to hear a sob-story about yours. So you can say, 'There's a delay because I can't get Simpsons to give me their figures', but then leave it at that. The truth here is that you should find a way to prevent such misunderstandings – in this instance you could have warned your colleague that you were having problems getting the figures – so although the root problem may not be your fault, you're responsible at least for poor communication.

- In the end, people who are angry want a result. So once you've shown that you understand their anger, offer a solution. For example, tell them you'll go to another supplier for prices, or that you'll get onto Simpsons again and if there's no result in 48 hours, you'll get back to your colleague about it. If there's also a poor communication problem, acknowledge this and show that it won't happen again. So you might say, 'I'll get onto Simpsons again, and I'll try to get prices out of Sergeants too, and Burkes. I'll have figures from at least one of them for you by Tuesday. And I can see now that I should have warned you that Simpsons were letting me down; another time I'll tell you in good time if I can't meet the deadline.'

If the other person's anger is justified, you'll find once you've been through these steps they will calm down because there's nothing left for them to be angry about. You've appreciated the seriousness of the problem, acknowledged their anger, agreed a solution and shown that it won't happen again.

A promise is a promise

If you've agreed a solution with someone, you must stick to your side of it. If you encounter problems, say so before it's too late and get their input into how to deal with it. Otherwise their anger will be even more justified next time.

Tactical anger

While some people's anger is genuine, others use anger as a weapon to intimidate you into giving in to them. This is a particularly difficult emotion to handle when it comes from someone who is already in a position of authority over you, such as your boss or the head of another department who is senior to you. Obviously this means they don't need to use such tactics to get you to carry out the tasks it is your job to do; a simple instruction is enough. But what about using anger to intimidate you into, for instance:

Some people use anger as a weapon to intimidate you into giving into them.

- doing tasks you're not obliged to;
- working longer hours than your contract stipulates;
- backing ideas you don't agree with;
- handling other people – perhaps your own subordinates – in ways you don't feel comfortable with;
- misleading other people on their behalf, or even lying to cover for them.

People use anger tactically because they have found it works. Like small children throwing tantrums, they probably discovered at an early age that they could get what they want this way, and they've kept on using the tactic ever since. The way to counter this is to let them see that this approach doesn't work on you. This means you'll have to be assertive (see Chapter 2), and not give in to them when they treat you in this way. Eventually (I can't pretend it works overnight), they'll realize they're wasting their breath and they'll stop using this tactic with you.

The assertive approach to handling tactical anger means refusing to allow it in your presence.

- Say something like, 'I'm not prepared to be shouted at, and I shall leave if you don't calm down.'

- If they don't stop, carry out your threat: leave the room. You can say, 'I'll talk to you when you're calmer', or simply say, 'Excuse me', and go.

- If they repeat the outburst at the next encounter, repeat your response to it. Keep on doing this until they learn to deal with you calmly and rationally.

> **The assertive approach to handling tactical anger means refusing to allow it in your presence.**

There's no denying that a lot of people find the prospect of talking to the boss, especially, in this way somewhat scary to say the least. But once the boss starts behaving like this, you're actually dealing with a five year old, not a manager. They may be senior to you in the organization, but on a personal level we're all equals, and you have the right to be treated respectfully.

There's nothing a senior manager can do to you for standing up to them; if they try other emotional games with you, you can simply respond assertively to those too. But in fact, it shouldn't come to that – if you've built an otherwise good relationship with this person, they will learn quickly not to use this tactic on you. They will respect you more for defending your rights calmly but firmly than they did when you used to buckle under the force of their anger.

> **On a personal level we're all equals, and you have the right to be treated respectfully.**

Feedback techniques (see later in this chapter) also work well in convincing someone to drop this unconstructive behaviour. One of the advantages of feedback is that it enables you to raise the issue at a time when the other person is not angry, so it can be resolved calmly and reasonably. You could use feedback to let them know that in future you won't remain in the room if they start shouting at you.

> **Positive spiral**
>
> One of the many reasons for managing other people well and build-ing a strong working relationship is that it makes it far easier to deal with issues like tactical anger employed against you. Refusing to give in can give rise to all sorts of unpleasantness if you do it in the con-text of a tricky relationship. But when you've built a relationship that is otherwise sound, honest and trusting, the other person will respond positively when you decline to play their game.

Sulking

In many ways, sulking is an alternative to anger. Most children tend towards either tantrums or sulking; few regularly use both. Many of us opt for one or the other in our personal relationships, too, when our emotions get the better of us. The same goes for those adults who are not mature enough to keep their displays of emotion away from their work.

People sulk because they want to let you know how upset they are. If they didn't sulk (they feel), you would think the matter wasn't important to them. Many of us are prone to sulk occasionally, but some people do it over such seemingly minor issues that it ends up happening frequently and creates an unpleasant and unhelpful attitude that can seriously sour the working relationship. When you have a col-league or a boss who is a sulker, things can get very unpleasant, so here are a few tips for handling it.

People sulk because they want to let you know how upset they are.

- Silence is intended to make you feel guilty once you realize how upset or disappointed in you the other person is. Any approach to handling a sulker only works if you honestly have nothing to feel guilty about. So when you have the kind of discussion with someone that can lead to an unpleasant silence, make sure you genuinely listen to them with an open mind, explain the reasons behind your view of the matter, and act in a friendly and reasonable way. Once the discussion is over, if they choose to sulk, you know that there is nothing else you could have done except give in for no good reason, simply to avoid the sulks.

- The aim is that you will capitulate. Never, ever do so. Just like using tactical anger, if it works for them once, they will try it every time.

The aim is that you will capitulate. Never, ever do so.

- Don't perpetuate the atmosphere by being short with them either. If they give you the silent treatment, just say, 'OK, we'll sort it out later.' Then behave as if everything were normal, and as though they weren't sulking at all. Don't be tempted to try to cheer them up, or keep checking if they're OK. Sooner or later, they'll have to abandon the tactic when it becomes clear that it simply isn't working.

Check the facts

Remember that most of us sulk to some extent over major issues when we believe our feelings aren't being taken seriously. Even frequent sulkers occasionally have a genuine case – they really aren't being listened to or considered over something important. So always make a mental check when they get upset and satisfy yourself that this isn't one of those occasions – or if it is, hear them out.

Tears

You're most likely to encounter tears from your subordinates when you give them bad news or discipline them. Occasionally you will encounter tears from your colleagues. When tears aren't genuine, they're a form of emotional blackmail (which we'll look at in a moment). When they are genuine, however, they can still be tricky to deal with until you know how. So here are the tactics you need to employ.

When tears aren't genuine, they're a form of emotional blackmail.

- If someone needs to cry, let them. You should have a box of tissues handy if there's any chance of tears, and offer it to them.

- Let them talk if they need to, and listen to them fully (see Chapter 6).

- You shouldn't consider changing the bad news (even if it's in your power) or retracting the disciplinary process, but you can ask them whether they'd like a break and to continue the discussion later. If so, offer to leave the room while they recover, assuming they would prefer this to walking out into a crowded office in their present state.

- The politically correct approach is not to put an arm round their shoulder or give them a hug. The human response might be quite different. So trust your instinct, but if in doubt, avoid physical contact. If you've just disciplined them, they're unlikely to want your sympathy. But if you've broken them the bad news that your boss has turned down your recommendation to promote this person, they may appreciate it. Take into account how well you know them, your social relationship (if any), and your respective sexes. And remember you also have the option of asking, 'Do you need a hug?'

- Just because they're upset, it doesn't mean they can't make their own decisions. So don't start doling out advice.

- Maintain the person's confidence, and don't tell anyone else that they broke down, or what was said.

Just occasionally you may encounter tears from your boss. Some bosses are very sensitive, others are going through particularly major emotional upheavals. Whether your boss has just been bawled out by the MD, or whether they are going through a particularly horrendous divorce, what do you do if they burst into tears in front of you? Here are a few guidelines.

- Drop the boss/subordinate relationship for the duration, and treat them as you would any fellow human being who is upset.

- If you think they might prefer you not to be there, ask them, 'Would you like me to leave?' If you don't get a direct answer, stay with them unless the signals to go are strong.

- Let them talk, and you do the listening.

- Don't give them any advice unless they specifically ask for it, and preferably not then either.

- Next time you see the boss you can ask, 'How are you feeling?', but don't make a big thing of it, or ask them repeatedly, unless they encourage it.

They may well be embarrassed later, and feel uncomfortable with any reference to it.

- No matter what they say or do, don't mention the incident to anyone else in or connected with the organization. Your boss will appreciate and respect your ability to maintain their confidence, and it will build their trust in you. Betraying their confidence will do serious damage to your relationship.

> **Don't give your boss any advice unless they specifically ask for it, and preferably not then either.**

- Unless your boss is also a close friend, don't mention the incident to them again unless they bring it up first. Most particularly, don't use it as any kind of emotional leverage. In other words, don't remind them how sympathetic you were just as you're asking for a day off, or imply that they owe you a favour.

Emotional blackmail

'I'm going to be in a real mess if you don't help me out with this.' 'Don't give me a hard time for being late – I find it so difficult to get up in the mornings.' 'Please don't be unco-operative.' Emotional blackmail is a popular weapon for getting people to do whatever the blackmailer wants. They are playing on your guilt, or your desire to be popular, in order to manipulate you into doing things their way.

> **There's one thing you need to know about emotional blackmail: it doesn't work on assertive people.**

But there's one thing you need to know about emotional blackmail: it doesn't work on assertive people. And emotional blackmailers learn to recognize assertive people and they then stop using this insidious technique on them. So apply a bit of assertiveness (Chapter 2) and become impervious to this kind of manipulation.

- Recognize emotional blackmail for what it is. As soon as you start to feel guilty about saying no, or emotionally uncomfortable about your response to someone, ask yourself, 'Am I being emotionally blackmailed?' Once you're alert to the possibility, you'll have no trouble recognizing when it's happening.

- Tell yourself that emotional blackmail is not a fair, equal, adult behaviour, and that you owe nothing to those who use it. If they're prepared to use such an underhand approach with you, you are quite entitled to respond by not giving in to it.

- Now simply stand your ground, according to the assertiveness guidelines in Chapter 2. If they persist, adopt the stuck record technique. Don't allow them to make you feel bad – it is they who are behaving unreasonably, not you.

- Challenging people directly over this technique can cause unpleasantness, but with some people you may find that you can say – with a joke and a laugh – 'Careful! That's starting to sound like emotional blackmail . . . ' It pulls them up short. If they think you're getting wise to them, they'll back off.

Feedback

Feedback is a specific technique for addressing problems with other people in a non-confrontational way. One of the big advantages of this is that it's a relatively easy way to approach someone, so you don't have to wait until you're at breaking point before you tackle them. It's a useful technique for dealing with colleagues, bosses and subordinates (and it even works outside work, too).

Feedback works especially well with persistent problems, which is what you tend to encounter with difficult people.

Feedback works especially well with persistent problems, which is what you tend to encounter with difficult people. Suppose you have someone on your team who is a persistent complainer. Talk to them in private, when neither of you is in a particular hurry. Here's how you can use the rules of feedback to resolve the problem.

1   Decide in advance what the key points you want to make are, and prepare ways of saying them that do not include:

- exaggeration, such as, 'you're always complaining';
- judgements, such as, 'you're hopeless at dealing with problems yourself';
- labels, such as, 'you're a whinger'.

2   When you speak to the person, focus on yourself and not them. Don't start sentences with 'You make me feel . . . '; try saying, 'I feel . . . when you . . . ' For example, 'I feel helpless and frustrated when you complain about things that I feel are minor details.'

3   Explain why you feel this way: 'I can't deal with them myself because I have other claims on my time which take higher priority; but I feel helpless having to say no to you.'

4   Now let the other person have their say. Listen to them, and show you're listening.

5   Focus on how they *behave,* not what they (in your view) *are.*

6   Be prepared to quote actual instances wherever possible.

The bigger picture

If the person you are talking to is a member of your team, relate their behaviour to the task: point out how their behaviour is impairing the team's ability to get results.

---

7   Suggest a solution and see how the other person feels. You must have an alternative behaviour in your mind that you are asking them to adopt – if you can't think of any solutions, you'd be better off not tackling the matter in the first place. Remember, you're not asking them to stop being a complaining person – they can't do that – you're asking them (perhaps not in so many words) to be a complainer who doesn't complain about certain things or at certain times. For example: 'Could you suggest a solution when you explain the problem to me? Try to think of something that doesn't involve time or resources that aren't available. Then when you talk to me I'll be better able to help and you'll find the complaint is more likely to be dealt with effectively.'

8   Listen to the other person's response and be prepared to compromise with them. (You may even learn something about how *you* appear to them, and be able to adapt your own behaviour and improve your performance.)

Give them the good news

When dealing with your own team, be positive as well. Tell them when they have done well by not complaining (or whatever the problem behaviour is). Show them they *can* behave co-operatively.

Many difficult people can be handled simply by using assertive behaviour (see Chapter 2) or with the techniques set out earlier in this chapter. But when these approaches don't get you the results you want, you can use feedback with any problem to meet your objective of resolving it swiftly and permanently, in a way which meets work objectives and satisfies everyone involved.

Summary

It's far easier to get what you want at work if you know how to handle difficult behaviour from other people. Whether it's anger or emotional blackmail, sulking or tears, an adult approach will give you the moral high ground every time without riling anyone.

- Keep calm and handle your own emotional response maturely.
- Apologize and make reparation in the face of justified anger.
- Refuse to give in to tactical anger.
- Ignore sulking.
- Be sympathetic to genuine tears without changing course.
- Don't give in to emotional blackmail.
- Use feedback to deal with persistent behaviour problems.

CHAPTER FIVE

Impress your boss

Your working relationship with your boss is almost certainly the most important relationship you have at work. Your boss is in a stronger position than anyone else to give you what you want (or withhold it) – from allocating the responsibilities or contracts you want, to awarding pay rises, perks and promotions. They have power over your colleagues as well as you, and influence with their own bosses. So it's in your best interests to work well with your boss and create a relationship that your colleagues will envy and your boss will treasure.

> **Your working relationship with your boss is almost certainly the most important relationship you have at work.**

You'll find here the top ten dos and don'ts for creating a truly terrific working relationship with your boss. These are all tips which will earn you extra brownie points with your boss. They're not about crawling or sucking up to the boss, but are all about simply working in a way which will make their life easier and more pleasant – and it will all be down to you.

Do . . .

1 . . . be popular

This doesn't mean you have to be a creep, nor even that you should never be tough – sometimes that's necessary. The point is that you should always be polite and courteous to everyone you encounter, and show appreciation when others are helpful to you; if you do this you are bound to be popular and well liked.

Your boss will notice the way you treat other people, and will be far more impressed if you are always pleasant to everyone than if you are rude or off-hand with people who are below you on the ladder. You also need to be courteous with colleagues, customers and other contacts. Your boss's life will be a whole lot easier if other people are happy to deal with you and do business with you.

You need to be courteous with colleagues, customers and other contacts.

Being popular to do business with is not only a matter of being civil to the people you deal with. It also means giving them good service. So whoever you're dealing with, customers or junior colleagues from other departments, follow a code of practice.

- Always reply to messages promptly.
- Always return phone calls when you say you will.
- Always meet any commitments you make (so don't make any you won't be able to meet).

These simple practices are very important because they send a message to the person concerned that you take them seriously. If you don't reply to someone's messages, call them when you said you would, or fulfil your commitments to them, you are in effect telling them they're not worth the bother. Earn yourself a reputation for being popular, considerate and polite, and your boss will feel confident in asking you to deal with other people.

2 . . . be willing to do a little extra

Any boss is grateful to have someone on the team who is happy to put themselves out from time to time. Even if home commitments mean you can never work overtime, it doesn't mean you can't show willing in other ways during normal hours.

Suppose there's a bug going round and you're short-staffed. Someone is needed to provide emergency cover on the sales desk for the morning, or to sit on reception over lunch. If you volunteer, it shows the boss you're enthusiastic about the job and that you want to make other people's lives a little easier (including theirs).

There are plenty of opportunities to give a little more than your job description commits you to, from helping out another department to agreeing to write an article for the next issue of the company newsletter. Apart from the helpfulness of actually doing the task, being a willing volunteer also saves your boss the time and stress of having to nag the team into helping.

There are plenty of opportunities to give a little more than your job description commits you to.

3 . . . identify with the organization

If you're a true corporate player, you will be rooting for the organization and enjoying its successes. When things are going well in the company, the division or the department, you'll be cheering along, part of the team yourself. Your boss will be pleased to see that you feel involved and loyal to the organization.

The alternative is to regard the organization as a separate entity, as many people do. They refer to the company as 'them' rather than 'us', and treat its successes as though they had happened to an organization unconnected with them. If you do this, you effectively indicate to your boss that you don't feel any loyalty to the organization, and that you don't care about it. Since your job is ultimately to bring the greatest possible benefit to the organization, it's hard to see quite how you'll be motivated to do this when you feel no attachment to it.

Make sure that you recognize that what is good for the organization is good for you too.

So make sure your boss can see that you are part of the family, and that you recognize that what is good for the organization is good for you too.

Us and them

Some organizations have an 'us' and 'them' culture, in which most employees regard senior management as being apart from them, and sometimes speak of them disparagingly or even contemptuously. As a general rule, it is the fault of senior management if this kind of culture is allowed to thrive. Nevertheless, if you work in this kind of company you can still make yourself the exception rather than the rule. It will make your boss's job easier, and will give the impression that you really belong.

4 . . . take criticism well

Any reasonable boss will criticize you only when they believe it's justified. More often than not, they're probably right. Many people react very defensively to being criticized and try to justify their actions. Some even get angry or upset. These reactions make it hard for the boss to encourage someone to grow and learn from their mistakes, and make them dread having to give criticism to such people – even though they know it's their job to do so.

How much more pleasant the boss's job will be if their constructive criticism is met by a mature and relaxed response. If you can provide this, you'll make yourself very popular. What you need to do is:

- Admit any mistakes or shortcomings. Not only is it a sign of strength to be able to do this, but it also reassures the boss that you are fully aware of where you've gone wrong.

- Show your boss appreciation for bringing your mistake to your attention. You can say something like, 'Thanks for pointing that out to me. I've learnt something useful, and I'll be able to do better next time.'

Admit any mistakes or shortcomings. It is a sign of strength to be able to do this.

Your boss will be relieved and impressed by your maturity and your strength of character in being able to handle criticism so well.

5 . . . write competently

We can't all write brilliantly, but we should all be able to write competently. A poor writing style will show up every time you write an e-mail or memo, let alone a report or proposal or a longer document. To those who cannot write or spell, this may be acceptable, but if your boss and other superiors can write competently, they will be disappointed in you. They will be wary of showing anything you've written to other people because it will reflect badly on the department and the organization.

So if your writing isn't up to scratch, you need to brush up on it. Learn how to write better by going to evening classes, reading books on how to write, or getting a friend or colleague to coach you. In the meantime, here are a few pointers to improving your writing style.

- Don't try to impress your readers with long words and jargon, or cleverly constructed sentences. You will only come across as pompous, and you're more likely to make mistakes. Aim for simple but clear writing, and short sentences. Not only does this read better, it's also far easier to achieve if writing isn't your strong point.

- Good layout is important, as well as spelling, grammar and punctuation. You will give an instantly favourable impression if any document, from a letter to a report, is well laid out and looks professional. Don't cram each page full of text, but leave comfortable margins and space around headings.

- For longer documents, use plenty of subheadings, bullet-pointed lists and short paragraphs (they should be wider on the page than they are deep) to make the material look interesting and approachable.

- If you've written an important document, get someone whose writing, spelling and grammar are good to check it through for you.

- Don't rely on computer spellcheckers. They're great for a first sweep through a piece of writing, but they miss a great deal of mistakes. They will tell you only if you write something that isn't a word. But many spelling mistakes result in genuine words that simply aren't the right ones. For example, if you miss the final 'f' from 'off', the computer will see a real word, 'of', and not correct it. So by all means use a spellchecker for an initial round of corrections, but check through the piece yourself, or get someone else to do it, as well.

Moving up the ladder

Many people get key promotions as a result of reports they've written, partly because reports – good ones at least – tend to be circulated around the higher echelons of the organization so they get you noticed. This is one reason why your writing style is so important. You don't want to produce a report with brilliant content but which fails to impress as it should because it's so poorly written.

---

6 . . . be open-minded

Organizations can only grow by changing. Paradoxically, change is a constant feature of most successful companies. So the job of management – including your boss – means spending a lot of time driving through change. One of the most frustrating things for bosses is finding that their team members resist the kind of changes they need to promote. Team members who are open to change and happy to embrace it are therefore highly popular with their bosses. What's more, if you can welcome change, it marks you out as being management material compared with those who instinctively resist it.

If you can welcome change, it marks you out as being management material compared with those who instinctively resist it.

Being open to change doesn't simply mean agreeing to go along with it, although that's a good start. If you really want to be seen as an open-minded member of the team, you can actively promote change, suggest new ideas and help to find ways to make any necessary changes work well. That way, you're not simply cheering from the sidelines, you're in the thick of the change game.

7 . . . accompany every problem with a solution

Some people just complain, complain, complain. They can't deliver this order on time because there's always a bottleneck in despatch. They don't see how this idea can work because it'll cost too much. They don't want to invite this client for a meeting because there's nowhere suitable in the building to meet.

If you're seen as this kind of persistent complainer, you'll frustrate your boss and gain a reputation for being negative and unconstructive. In a way it can seem unfair: maybe there *is* always a bottleneck in despatch. Or the idea on the table *is* too costly. Or there *isn't* a presentable meeting room. So what are you supposed to do? Keep quiet about it and let the problems continue?

Of course not. All you have to do is to come up with a solution. Not a sarcastic, obviously flawed one ('I'll just get on the plane to Bahrain and deliver it myself, shall I, since despatch can't seem to get it there?'). You need to find a solution that is better than the present option, even if it isn't perfect. For example:

- Post the urgent package first class yourself, and then offer to work with despatch to propose a solution to their bottleneck problems.
- Suggest ways in which the costly idea could be modified to bring the costs down, or ways in which the money could be found to finance it.
- Explain the problem with the lack of suitable meeting rooms and ask to take the clients out for a lunch meeting instead. Then recommend a feasible way to turn one of the offices into an occasional meeting room that could be made smart and presentable.

By doing this you are drawing your boss's attention to exactly the same problem, but you're doing it in a way that makes you look like a fixer, a problem-solver, a solutions person. In other words, just the kind of person your boss wants at their right hand. So the rule is simple: every time you bring a problem or complaint to your boss's attention, couple it with a workable solution.

> **Add to the fun**
>
> If you get into the habit of looking for solutions yourself rather than presenting problems to others and expecting them to solve them, you'll soon find that your whole outlook on work becomes more positive, and you start to see difficulties as challenges rather than problems. You may well find this change of emphasis means that you enjoy work far more, and find it more motivating than before.

8 . . . praise but don't flatter

What's the difference between praise and flattery? If you are sincere, genuine and in proportion in your remarks, you are praising. If you are insincere or excessive in your praise, it becomes empty flattery.

Your boss needs praise just as much as you do. Maybe they get it from their boss or maybe they don't, but either way their boss isn't in such close proximity to them as you are. So they're bound to miss a lot of praiseworthy actions. However, you can fill in the gaps by making sure that you give your boss praise when it's due.

Your boss needs praise just as much as you do.

You want to be certain that you come across as being genuine and not as a creep. Apart from anything else, once your praise turns (or appears to turn) to empty flattery, it ceases to be worth anything to your boss. To make sure this doesn't happen, consider the following:

- Praise your boss only when you genuinely mean it.
- Don't go over the top. A simple, 'I liked the way you handled that', or 'Hmm. Impressed!' is often sufficient.
- Save the really strong praise for those big successes that come only occasionally – clinching a major contract or solving a serious problem.
- If your boss's achievement is shared with anyone else, distribute your praise to everyone involved, don't just focus on the boss.

9 . . . be loyal

We've already touched on loyalty to the organization, which is certainly important. But of course you also need to show loyalty to your boss personally, not only in their presence but also when they're not there – in front of the team, other colleagues, senior management, customers and suppliers. In other words, loyalty is a permanent thing. You can't pick it up sometimes and drop it at others.

> **Loyalty is a permanent thing. You can't pick it up sometimes and drop it at others.**

On a personal level, loyalty to the boss means no gossiping about them behind their back, on personal or professional topics. Sometimes there may be a genuine need to discuss the boss with your immediate colleagues, but make sure you say nothing that is unfair, unjustified or irrelevant to the discussion. In particular, never give away any confidence about the boss, no matter what. And your boss shouldn't have to tell you that something is confidential. Suppose they confided in you once that their marriage was shaky; this kind of information should automatically be treated as confidential. Even if a colleague tells you that the boss told them too, that still doesn't entitle you to divulge any details which may have been given to you alone.

Loyalty to your boss means not only resisting gossip and criticism, but also actively backing them up. Some bosses don't make this easy for you; nevertheless if one of your boss's fellow managers criticizes the boss in front of you, you need to stand up for them. Remember, the other manager may disagree with you, but privately they'll be thinking, 'I hope my team members would stick up for me like that.'

Another aspect of loyalty is backing up the boss in front of them when they're being attacked by others. Obviously in the line of amicable discussion of, say, a new idea, you should feel free to express your personal opinion (unless your boss asks you to do otherwise). But if things turn unpleasant or personal, or other people are criticizing your boss's past actions, you need to give them all your support. If you share some of the other people's views, you can say so privately to your boss later if you wish. But in public, showing loyalty is more important than voicing your personal opinion.

Careless talk

As a rule of thumb, before you say anything about your boss, ask yourself how you would feel if it got back to them. If you're making a genuine, relevant and fair criticism in front of friends, you should be able to justify it easily to the boss if ever you had to. But if you feel uncomfortable at the thought of having to justify remarks made out of place – either unfair comments, or fair but made to the wrong people – then bite your tongue.

10 . . . under-promise and over-deliver

This is a great rule for dealing with everyone, and especially bosses. Not only does it prevent you disappointing people by letting them down, it goes further and gives you the chance actively to impress the boss and anyone else you apply it with.

The principle is very simple. You promise less than you feel you should be able to manage. So if your boss asks you to complete a task by Friday and you reckon you can do it by Wednesday, you keep quiet about your own assessment and you simply agree to Friday. Then, when all goes to plan, you're done by Wednesday and you deliver more than you promised – the task's done *and* it's two days early. What's more, if your world happens to collapse round your ears earlier in the week, you've built in two days' leeway and you should still complete the task on time – by Friday.

This approach can't fail to impress. Often you'll be asked to say when you can complete a task. Never give the earliest time you think you can manage – you will only disappoint if things go wrong and you're late. Always give the latest you feel is acceptable and that your boss will agree to. Then your *worst* scenario is that you still meet the deadline. Very often we're talking about shorter timescales. Tell the boss you can get something done in an hour when you know it should only take half an hour. Tell them you'll get back to them with figures after lunch when you hope you should have them ready by mid-morning. This way, you're constantly setting yourself up to impress.

This works with things other than deadlines; it also applies to standards. For example, you might tell the boss you can get the figures for this year by the end of the day, but you won't have the last three years' figures until tomorrow. Privately you reckon you should have them all by 5 o'clock, but you're building in some leeway, and the boss will be delighted if your private view is right and you've got the whole lot by close of play today.

Or you might tell your boss that when you negotiate the upcoming deal with one of your suppliers, you reckon you can get the discount you're after, but that quality guarantees may not improve. Privately, you're hoping to get an increase in quality guarantees too.

Don't . . .

1 . . . splash out on expenses

Nobody expects you to forego your business expenses, but the way that you use your expense account says a lot about you. If you spend the most you can get away with, always taking customers out for expensive meals, or staying at the best hotels, the implication is that:

- you are extravagant and don't know the value of money;
- you can barely be trusted with a budget;
- you're happy to fleece the company; and
- you don't care about your boss's budget constraints.

None of these says a lot for you as an employee. If, on the other hand, you're sensible with your expenses and can easily justify everything you spend, you'll look reliable, trustworthy and loyal. So don't book into the grottiest cheap hotel, or take your customers for lunch at the local greasy spoon, but do show moderation and your boss will notice and appreciate it.

If you're sensible with your expenses, you'll look reliable, trustworthy and loyal.

> **Risking your reputation**
>
> The closer you come to overspending your expense account, the greater danger there is that your boss will start to question why you're spending so much. There's an increasing danger that they will suspect that you may be fiddling some claims. Even if they can't prove it (very possibly because you're not doing it), they will be left with lingering doubts about your honesty.

2 . . . badmouth your ex-boss

When you speak critically of an ex-boss, what do you suppose your present boss thinks? Do you imagine they feel sorry for you working for such a difficult manager, and resolve to make your life more pleasant in future? No, they don't. Here's what they actually think:

- 'There are two sides to every story. I wonder what really happened?'
- 'Is this what they'll be saying about me once I become their ex-boss?'
- 'What a negative attitude. If they haven't got anything good to say, they shouldn't say anything at all.'

The fact is that all your comments about your ex-boss may be entirely justified – understated even – but that's not the impression you'll give to your present boss. Every impression you can give to them is a poor one, so don't badmouth the ex-boss, whether they're from this organization or a different one.

Badmouthing the last organization you worked for shows disloyalty.

The same goes for your ex-company. Badmouthing the last organization you worked for (or any others) shows disloyalty and makes your boss wonder what you'll be saying about this company in a few years' time.

3 . . . complain about menial tasks

From time to time, we all need to do tasks outside our normal routine which some might consider beneath them. Whether the boss asks you to fetch extra chairs, cover on reception at lunchtime, or stuff envelopes, you need to show that you're happy to perform these tasks.

Your boss wouldn't be asking you to do these things unless there were a good reason. Maybe there's some kind of crisis under way, or perhaps you're seriously short-staffed. If you say no to doing them, you give the impression of being arrogant and full of your own importance. More importantly, however, you also show that you've missed the point.

Your boss is looking at the bigger picture: the immediate priority is simply to get the chairs moved before the customers arrive. Who actually does the job is secondary. If you won't co-operate, you're demonstrating that you aren't capable of seeing where the team's priorities lie, but can only see your own narrow role. If, however, you muck in cheerfully, you show the boss that you are a real team player who, like them, has an eye on the bigger issue.

4 . . . bear grudges

You cannot work effectively as part of a team if you sulk when you're put out, or if you bear grudges. Your boss will quickly become frustrated with anyone who upsets the team's balance and morale by creating an atmosphere or allowing disagreements to fester.

You cannot work effectively as part of a team if you sulk when you're put out.

If you are unhappy with your boss, a team mate or any close working colleague, either address the problem or forget about it. But whatever you do, don't bear a grudge.

5 . . . go over your boss's head

One surefire way to irritate your boss is to go direct to their boss without consulting them first. It's disrespectful and it undermines their authority. It also implies that you don't think they know their job, and you're telling their boss so too. Altogether not very surprising, then, if it damages your relationship with them severely.

Clearly this rule applies to complaining about your workload or even about your boss. But it also applies to putting forward ideas. If you have an important proposal to make, take it to your boss before you show it to any other managers, and let *them* be the one to take it forward.

Diplomacy first

If you feel strongly that you have no option but to go direct to your boss's boss, think hard about alternative approaches. One compromise solution can be to go to several managers simultaneously, including your own boss. For example, you might copy other managers in on an e-mail to your boss if you're warning of the dangers of a decision which you believe will be catastrophic for the organization and you can't convince the boss without their support. Even so, you should avoid this approach unless you have exhausted all other possibilities first.

---

6 . . . confront the boss in front of other people

Never wash your dirty linen in public. If you're unhappy with your boss, save it until the two of you can discuss it in private. Your boss will never forgive you if you embarrass or humiliate them in front of other people, and you'll look pretty shoddy yourself to the people who witness your outburst.

Your boss will never forgive you if you embarrass or humiliate them in front of other people.

It doesn't matter how justified you are in your complaint, you are never justified in making it public. Bite your tongue if necessary and don't let your anger or frustration out until the appropriate time – which won't be until you've calmed down anyway.

7 . . . repeat mistakes

It's natural to make mistakes, and your boss knows that. Great scientists such as Thomas Edison, Linus Pauling and Albert Einstein all believed that you couldn't achieve successes without notching up failures on the way.

What the likes of Edison and Einstein did, however, was to make sure they never made the same mistake twice. That is a waste of time and teaches you nothing. Each time you make a mistake you need to learn from it so that you are closer to the next success.

Your boss expects you to make mistakes, but also expects you to learn from them. They want to know that if you've got something wrong once, they can count on you never to get it wrong again. So make sure you don't repeat your mistakes, and reassure your boss by being clear that you know where you've gone wrong and can prevent it recurring. For example, 'I can see now that if I'd phoned to confirm the booking I'd have found out in time that there was a problem, so I need to do that in future. Whenever I make a booking I'll put a note in my diary for nearer the time to phone and confirm it. That way, this can't happen again.'

8 . . . gossip

We've already established that you shouldn't bitch about your boss or your ex-boss. But you don't want to get yourself a name as a gossip generally. Gossip is far more common and damaging in organizations where communication is poor than in those which communicate well. But even in well-run companies, gossip about the organization is the bane of management's life.

Gossip about the organization is the bane of management's life.

Rumours can fly round an organization – closures, lay-offs, big changes for better or worse – and can do a huge amount of damage to management/staff relations. Don't be a part of this, or you'll be branded a troublemaker.

Ask for clarification

If there's a rumour going round about critical decisions or changes to the organization, your best bet is to go to the boss yourself. Don't mention names or get the gossips into trouble. Just explain that you thought management should know what is being said, and should be warned that if they don't communicate the correct facts to their employees, the gossip is likely to get worse. Doing this sets you apart from the gossips (despite the fact that you've obviously been listening to them), and supports management without getting any of your colleagues into trouble.

Gossip about other people in the organization is far less damaging to management as a rule (unless it's about them), but your boss is unlikely to draw the same distinction you do between different types of gossip. If you're labelled a gossip, you're labelled a gossip and that's that. And your boss will think that you rumour-monger or bitch about them even if you don't. The only safe course is to steer well clear of the gossips round the coffee machine, and be seen to be above all that.

9 . . . bother your boss when they're busy

Your boss doesn't only have you to bother them when they're busy. They have a whole team of people to pester them at inconvenient moments. Wouldn't it be nice to be the one your boss could count on to leave them alone just when they need it most?

Learn to recognize when your boss is busy or preoccupied, and don't disturb them. If they're completing a project to a tight deadline, or rushing to a meeting they're on the verge of being late for, give them a break. Here are some ways to make your interruptions as few and as convenient as possible.

● Anticipate problems so you have time to wait for a good moment to discuss them with the boss.

- Collect together several minor questions or discussion points and then disturb your boss just once to deal with all of them.

- If you phone your boss or stick your head round the door, always start by asking 'Have you got five minutes?', or 'Is this a good moment?'

- For anything that requires privacy or needs some time to discuss, make an appointment with the boss. However, don't irritate them by asking for meetings every other day – save it for the issues which really warrant it.

- Be aware of the pressures your boss is under so you can avoid disturbing them at times when they are very pressured.

If you follow all these guidelines, you'll almost never have to bother your boss at a difficult time. And when you do interrupt them, which will only be in genuinely urgent emergencies, your boss will know that you must have a valid reason to do it – unlike most of the rest of the team who pester them without consideration.

10 . . . upstage your boss

Your boss may be a shy retiring type or an egocentric megalomaniac. Either way, they like to be praised and given the limelight from time to time, even if they don't give the impression that they do. So make sure that when they are praised by other people, you don't get in the way.

This isn't the time to point out your contribution to the success in question, nor to mention how much luck the project needed to succeed. This is the time to help direct the focus on to your boss and their achievement. If they are magnanimous enough to mention that they couldn't have done it without the support of the team, that's great. If they aren't that generous . . . well, that's their prerogative. Comfort yourself with the fact that their success is bound to reflect well on the rest of you in any case.

CHAPTER SIX

Learn to listen

The idea of learning how to listen probably seems either unnecessary or patronizing. Surely we've all been doing it since we were babies? Well, yes, we've all been listening superficially – that is to say, hearing. But really listening carefully is a different skill, and one which we can still learn after we've grown up. So what's the point of learning to listen properly? Well, it has several benefits.

- It prevents mistakes caused by crossed lines and poor communication.
- It helps you understand what is going on.
- It enables you to read between the lines when someone is speaking to you.
- It makes the other person feel more positively towards you.

All of these are important in helping you to get what you want. Few of us are dreadful listeners (though we probably know one or two people who are), but most of us could listen better if we just learnt some of the basic techniques.

Two-way benefit

If you go through the motions of listening carefully, you'll find that without trying you really do listen better. Equally, if you listen carefully to begin with, you'll notice yourself following the guidelines in this chapter without even trying. Whether you approach this new set of skills by genuinely listening or by 'faking' it, you'll end up listening better than you did before. You can't lose.

Eliminate poor listening

To begin with, you need to do away with as many barriers to effective listening as you can. We all have them. There are times we listen better than others, and the worse times are generally the result of some block we have put up that inhibits our ability to listen properly. How many of these sometimes prevent you from listening as well as you might? (Be honest.)

- You're too busy planning your next response to take in what the other person is saying.

- You go off on a sidetrack train of thought sparked by something they said.

- You stop listening because you reckon you know what they're going to say.

- You are too preoccupied with thinking about how much you disagree to listen properly.

- You're simply listening out for an opportunity to butt in and say your piece.

- You get bored.

When you're listening to something you need to take in clearly, be conscious of any blocks you put up and simply remove them.

Once you learn to recognize these barriers when you put them up, it becomes much easier to take them down. So when you're listening to something you need to take in clearly, be conscious of any blocks you put up and simply remove them.

There's another set of barriers to good listening, and those are the ones that come from outside yourself. For example:

- You don't understand what the other person is saying – it's too complicated or they're using too much jargon.

- There are noises or distractions which are taking your attention.

- They are taking longer than you expected, and you're distracted because you're due in a meeting in two minutes.

- They are slow, long-winded, boring or rambling, or they keep repeating themselves.

Say that again?

Repetitious people can be very boring to listen to, to be honest. But why do you think they repeat themselves? It's often because they think they're not getting through to us. It's a vicious circle: they bore us so we don't listen, they sense we're not listening so they repeat themselves to get through to us, we become more bored . . . and so on. The solution is simple. If we listen properly in the first place, they'll have no need to repeat themselves, and everyone will benefit.

By and large, honesty is the best policy if you find you can't listen properly. For example:

- Tell the person you don't follow what they are saying. Ask them to explain it more clearly.
- Tell them if there are certain words you don't understand, and ask them to explain them to you.
- Let them know you are being distracted and ask to move somewhere where you can give them your full attention – it may be away from the door, or it might mean moving to another room.
- Explain that this is going to take longer than you thought, and you have to be somewhere else. Ask to get together later when you can concentrate better.

All these responses will actually flatter the person you're talking with, since they are all ways of telling them that you want the opportunity to listen to them better.

The exception to the 'be honest' rule is when the problem is personal – the person you're dealing with *is* boring, rambling or slow. In this case, it's not a good idea to say so straight out (no surprises there). By and large, you're just going to have to grin and bear it, and regard it as the ultimate training for good listening skills. However, you should find that when you practise effective listening, a lot of these barriers either reduce or become easier to tolerate.

Listening actively

Once you've dealt with the barriers to listening, you can start actively listening to the other person. A large part of this entails concentrating on what they are saying, and making sure none of those barriers can pop up and get in the way. Catch yourself as soon as your mind starts to wander, or you find yourself planning your counter-argument, and bring your mind back to what the other person is saying to you.

What's your point of view?

If you mentally view listening as an opportunity to improve your rapport with whoever is speaking, and to learn or gather information, you'll find active listening far easier than if you view it as an opportunity to put your own point of view. A simple change of attitude can vastly improve your listening skills.

It's important to let the other person know you're listening. It helps them establish that they're making themselves clear, as well as being polite and respectful. You'll also find that it's easier to concentrate and listen properly if you are focused on showing that you're listening. You can show your attention by various means:

- Making eye contact with the person who is speaking.
- Making encouraging noises, such as, 'Mmm', or 'Uh-huh', or 'Go on . . .'
- Making encouraging signs, such as smiling, nodding or leaning forwards.
- Repeating key phrases, such as, 'Deliver by Tuesday week, OK.'
- Paraphrasing important points, such as, 'So Richmonds can't go ahead with their launch unless we confirm the specifications this week.'

If you follow all these points you'll have to listen properly, and the other person will feel they have your full attention. In addition to making all these active indications that you're listening, there are other things you need to avoid if you're going to listen fully. In particular, don't:

- interrupt (tempted though you may be);
- keep asking for minor points of clarification – save them until the other person has finished speaking.

One useful technique is to make a conscious point of visualizing anything concrete that someone is telling you.

See it their way

One useful technique is to make a conscious point of visualizing anything concrete that someone is telling you. If they are explaining that the pink copies go to the accounts department, conjure up a mental image of one of the desks in accounts covered in piles of pink paper. If they are giving you directions, create a picture in your mind of yourself turning left at a newsagents, or right by a large tree, or whatever.

Silent signals

Some of the techniques for active listening involve using your own body language to show that you're listening – nodding, making eye contact and so on. But listening fully also entails taking in the body language signals that the person you're talking to is sending out – often unwittingly.

Our body language is almost always honest, unlike some of the words we use.

Our body language is almost always honest, unlike some of the words we use. We often say things we don't really mean, especially when it comes to talking about our feelings. We say things like, 'I'm not angry with you', or 'I'm not worried', when in fact we are.

If you're attuned to body language as well as spoken words, you should be able to tell when the person you're listening to is saying one thing and indicating another with their body language. When this happens, you can bet it's the body language that is telling the truth. Often we sense that something doesn't ring true but we're not clear what. When this happens, analyze the body language and see if it's out of synch with the words.

Reading body language isn't a specialized science – it's just a matter of being on the lookout for the signals. Here are a few examples of mixed messages that should alert you to the possibility of an unspoken subtext.

Words	Body language
'I'm confident we'll complete this project on time'	Strumming fingers, biting top lip
'I'm not angry'	Tense voice, leaning forward, clenching fist
'I'm really concerned to hear you're not happy'	Looking over your shoulder at something else, checking watch

I'm not suggesting that every one of these guarantees that the person you're talking to is lying to you. One or two minor contradictory actions or gestures may mean nothing. But a strong set of contradictions, especially coupled with a sixth sense on your part that what you're hearing doesn't ring true, is a good reason to suspect that you're not hearing the whole story.

Keep a weather eye on your skills

If you want to test how good you're getting at listening, here's a simple test you can do. Watch a three-minute weather broadcast, or listen to one on the radio, and see how much of it you can take in. Talk to the television (or radio) if it helps, repeating key phrases, for example, and then see how much of the broadcast you can repeat afterwards. You don't have to get the words exact, of course; the aim is to have absorbed the key points.

Getting other people to listen

If only everyone we deal with was as good at listening as they could be. And people who don't listen are often inclined to blame any lack of communication on you rather than on themselves. So here are some general pointers for getting the person you're talking to to listen to you properly.

People who don't listen are often inclined to blame any lack of communication on you rather than themselves.

- If you're talking to a poor listener, make sure you express yourself as succinctly and as briefly as you can. Make it as easy as possible for them to listen.

- Ask them to repeat key points to you: 'Can you say it back to me, just so I know I've made myself clear?' Often people can remember the last thing you said without having really taken it in; getting them to repeat it will fix it more clearly in their mind.

- Ask them questions as you go along. Try to ask open questions (which can't be answered in a single word or two but require more thought). For example, if you're trying to tell your boss you haven't got as much time as you feel you need for a project, you might ask, 'How would *you* tackle the research for this report with only a couple of days to do it in?'

Remember the written word

If you want people to remember what you've said to them, you don't have to rely wholly on their listening skills. Follow up important conversations with an e-mail or memo summarizing the key points.

If you follow all these guidelines you should find that active listening becomes a habit very quickly. And you'll soon get the hang of making poor listeners take more notice of what you're saying. So bad communication will become a thing of the past, you'll be clear what the unspoken messages are, and you'll be in a far better position to make sure you get what you want out of every conversation.

CHAPTER SEVEN

Manage meetings

One of the most effective forums for getting what you want at work is in a meeting. If you want something that requires the agreement of several people or departments, this is where the vital decisions will be made. If you need more resources, a change in the system or a new idea or product to be adopted, you'll need to convince a group of people at a meeting. And you can start working on getting what you want before the meeting begins.

> **One of the most effective forums for getting what you want at work is in a meeting.**

Talk to people

One of the key things you can do is talk to other people. This helps in a number of ways.

- *To find out their attitude to specific issues.* It helps to know whether all of the half dozen people in the meeting are going to agree with you or disagree, or what the split will be. There's no point spending hours preparing an argument if it turns out everyone agrees with you anyway. But there's a lot of point if you're going to be heavily outnumbered. And, of course, it's not just down to numbers. It makes a big difference which people are or aren't on your side. So sound out the other members of the meeting – at least the most influential ones – so you know what you're up against.

If you talk to people in advance of the meeting to find out who is and isn't in agreement with you, it will also help if you can find out what the arguments against you are. So if a colleague tells you, 'Actually, I'm dead against relocating the Essex office and moving them onto this site with us', ask them what their reasons are. You don't have to say you're preparing your case for the meeting – you're simply asking their view on a current issue. You may not even have to tell them you disagree – you could indicate that you're still deciding what you think is best.

- *To solicit their support.* If you can enlist your colleagues' support before the meeting, you know you won't be arguing your case alone. So talk to any likely prospects – take them for a drink or a bite of lunch – and get them on board.

- *To share resources.* You and your colleagues haven't got a lot of spare time even when you prepare in advance. So why spend hours doing all the research you need to back up your case alone? Get those of your colleagues who agree with your side of the argument to share out the preparation work – one of you can find out the prices of alternative options from the one being proposed, one of you can go online to find relevant statistics, one of you can talk to the staff to find out what their views are, one of you can dig out that article from last month's issue of *Business Week*, and so on.

Just make sure you don't rely on unreliable colleagues for essential information. You'll need to get together before the meeting to pool your resources and check that your facts don't contradict each other or undermine your argument.

Preserving loyalty

If you've persuaded someone round to supporting you at the meeting and you want to consolidate their support, ask them to help research the facts to back up the case. It will make it much harder for them to change sides when it comes to the meeting.

- *To find out information you need to present your case effectively.* Colleagues who are attending the meeting are not the only people you may need to talk to. It can lend huge weight to your case to be able to say, 'I've sounded out a few of our suppliers about this . . .', or 'I've talked to three of our other regional accounts managers to find out how they handle this . . .', or 'We've run a mini-survey among the staff in the transport department and they feel . . . ' So talk to anyone you can think of whose opinion or experience will lend support and credibility to your argument.

If this all sounds like a huge amount of work, bear in mind that you're not likely to have to do this for every agenda item at every meeting. Focus your time on getting the results that really matter to you. There may be only one controversial item on the agenda – or at least only one that you are particularly concerned about. And you may not need to research any background facts on it. Or perhaps you don't actually need to speak to other people – suppliers, customers, staff – about it. Some meetings require very little preparation time, although some are important and complex enough that you may want to put hours or even days into getting your preparation absolutely right.

Talk to anyone you can think of whose opinion or experience will lend support and credibility to your argument.

> **Don't run with the crowd**
>
> Remember that meetings are places to impress, as well as to get your point across. So dig up some information on key agenda items even if they're not controversial. Come up with facts (just one useful fact for one agenda item will do) that no one else has found. Don't pull data out of the accompanying papers that everyone has. Talk to an expert for two minutes, or go online and find some relevant statistics. Then impress everyone with information that only you have bothered – or thought – to unearth.

Preparing your case

In order to put your point across effectively and get what you want, you need facts and figures to back up your argument. So find them. It helps tremendously to have some idea of the arguments that will be levelled against you; that way you can direct your research where it is most useful.

The best way to decide what research needs doing is to list the key arguments you want to make in your favour. There will generally be up to about half a dozen of these. Suppose the issue in question is whether to relocate to larger offices, and you really want to stay where you are. Your arguments might be:

- huge upheaval resulting in a drop in productivity for several weeks;
- staff are opposed to the idea;
- no available site as convenient as this;
- move is unnecessary.

Now you want to think about the most convincing facts you could come up with to support each of these arguments, and then go and dig out the facts.

- *Huge upheaval resulting in low productivity.* Talk to other organizations or branches of your company which have relocated, and ask for their experiences, especially any figures on productivity during the move, and how long the effects lasted. Look for similar data on the Internet or in the trade press.

- *Staff are opposed to the idea.* Talk to the staff, or the managers concerned. Run a mini-poll if you can. Dig out letters or articles in staff publications. Get input from trade union reps.

- *No other site as convenient.* Compare this site with proposed locations for proximity to rail stations and main roads, convenience for staff, ease of recruiting staff, access for transport fleet, rush hour traffic flows and so on.

- *Move is unnecessary.* Find alternatives to avoid overcrowding present site. For example, demonstrate how certain departments could operate from their own site without posing communication problems, or how the present site could be utilized more effectively. Perhaps talk to a specialist architect or planner.

Decide what data will best support your argument, and then find it.

You get the picture. Decide what data will best support your argument, and then find it. The second stage of the process is to list the opposition's key arguments, and repeat the process for these, looking for data to refute the arguments. For example:

- present site is overcrowded;
- a purpose-built site will be more cost effective to run;
- current offices are shabby and run-down, and a new building will present a far better image for the organization.

In the first instance, as you can see, you have already done the research. But the second and third arguments raise points on which you can usefully dig out more facts and figures. For example, the cost of refurbishing the present buildings, or the ease of introducing more cost-effective practices at the existing site.

So to prepare your case, you must establish which facts and figures will most usefully

- *support* your case; and
- *refute* the case for the opposition.

Then dedicate your time to finding the information you need.

Getting your point across

You may have a valid case to put – possibly one that you feel is compelling – but somehow your colleagues don't always see it the same way. In fact, they sometimes barely let you express it at all. So how can you make the most of whatever time you are allotted, and be sure of making the most convincing case possible, while everyone else is actually listening to you?

As always, preparation is important. You may not get a chance to repeat yourself, and you may not get long to speak. So you need to be:

- clear; and
- succinct.

If you decide in advance what you want to say, you are far more likely to achieve these two objectives. So what you want is a simple formula for expressing yourself clearly and briefly. And, as luck would have it, I've got just the formula you need.

What you need to do is to compress the points you want to make into a kind of mini-presentation. It might take as little as 20 or 30 seconds in the relatively informal atmosphere of a meeting, but it should still follow the format of a presentation. After all, presentations are designed to put across an argument persuasively and with clarity, which is exactly what you are aiming for here (you'll find more guidelines on being persuasive in Chapter 12).

So here's the formula around which to prepare what you'll be saying:

1   Position

2   Problem

3   Possibilities

4   Proposal.

. . . a simple four-step process which you can apply to any argument you want to express at a meeting.

Book your place

If you're worried that you may not get a word in edgewise at this meeting – too many other people there who like the sound of their own voice – have a word with the chairperson before the meeting and say, for example, 'I've been doing some research into item 4 on the agenda, which I think will be very helpful to the meeting. Could you please see that I get a chance to outline it?'

Position

You need to start by clarifying the situation. This may take only half a sentence, but it is worth doing. Suppose the issue is over whether or not to move offices. You might start by saying, 'At the moment, the entire south west regional staff is based here at this site . . . ' You may feel you're stating the obvious, but it has several advantages.

- There may be people at the meeting for whom this is a new topic, and the basic facts may not be as obvious to everyone as you might think.

- This is the first step of expressing the issue in a nutshell. Encapsulating the whole issue for everyone in the space of a few sentences generates clarity – especially if the meeting has been talking round the issue and disappearing off on related sidetracks for some time. And it shows that you are one of those people who can step back and look at the big picture, something which will do your reputation no harm.

- However much disagreement there has been up until now, your opening couple of sentences will promote unity. You're all agreed what the position is – the debate is over what to do about it. It never hurts to get everyone to agree with you, even if it only lasts until you hit the controversial points.

- Just occasionally, there will be disagreement in the meeting over what the real issue or problem is. Summarizing it like this should bring any confusion out into the open and allow it to be resolved in order to tackle the real problem effectively.

Problem

Now it's time to go on and state why the current position won't do – why it needs to be addressed. For example, 'As the organization is growing, it's becoming increasingly difficult to fit everyone onto this site.' You're phrasing the problem in a way which everyone can agree with, but which maintains clarity and continues summarizing the issue in a nutshell.

Possibilities

You want to carry on being as uncontroversial as possible here, to maintain agreement and to deter interruptions. One important component of this is to sound as impartial as possible. This is an advantage because:

- It encourages everyone else to listen rather than argue, as they would with a biased or emotive statement.

- It makes you sound like the kind of balanced, rational person who can see all the sides of an argument. Not only will this impress your colleagues and superiors, but it also lends credibility to your proposed solution – it will be the proposal of someone who has weighed up all the facts logically, not someone who has barged in with a reflex emotional response.

- It means you are genuinely contributing a useful, succinct summary of the situation to help the meeting retain its clarity.

So you might summarize the possibilities by saying, 'There are three basic options: we move to a new site, we move *part* of the regional operation to a new site, or we stay here and adapt the present site to cope with the pressures of growth.' There. It's hard to see how anyone could reasonably take issue with that.

Let me finish . . .

If you don't want to be interrupted while you're speaking, here are two techniques which make it very hard for people to interrupt you without being downright rude.

1 State how many points you have to make: 'There are three reasons for this view . . . ' It's hard for people not to let you finish.

2 Breathe in mid-sentence, so you don't have to pause for breath at the end. That way, they don't get a look in unless they interrupt you in midstream.

Proposal

You've established an oasis of agreement in the midst of your meeting. Now it's time to state which of the possibilities you prefer. Again, you do this very simply, and you give your key arguments (the ones you prepared earlier) to justify your view. These are the key arguments which give you the best chance of getting the result you want.

For example: 'After looking at the options, I believe the best choice is to stay here for four key reasons. Firstly, my research shows that the upheaval involved in this kind of move tends to lead to an average drop in productivity of 50 per cent, lasting for up to three months. Secondly, the move would be unpopular with the staff, 67 per cent of whom are against it at the moment. Thirdly, this site is ideally located both for commuting access for staff and for key distribution routes. The two main alternative sites proposed are unpopular with employees – making recruitment harder – and one is in the middle of a particularly notorious rush hour congestion area. Finally, I understand that this site could be redesigned and refurbished at a lower cost than relocation. My figures show that with sound planning we could accommodate a 4 per cent growth for at least ten more years without expanding out of this site.'

Was that convincing, or was that convincing? You've been brief, clear and very persuasive. If anyone wants to question you, they'll find you can quote chapter and verse for all the figures you gave. If they try to bring counter-arguments, you've got data to refute those too. You've got your point across as effectively as you could have wished, and you won't have failed to impress anyone worth impressing in the process.

Prepare your mini-proposal well, and then ask a friend or colleague to rehearse you.

Screwing up courage

Meetings can be quite intimidating, especially if there are a lot of senior colleagues present, or maybe important customers. So prepare your mini-proposal well, and then ask a friend or colleague to rehearse you, and tell you how persuasive and well thought out it sounds. At worst you'll end up sounding good (which is plenty); at best you'll come across as brilliant.

Winning in debate

Once you've made your point initially, you're into the process of reinforcing it through debate and questioning. Or you may be responding to someone else's input. When you're into this stage of the meeting, there are a few tips you will find useful to help you sound convincing and persuasive, and give you the best chance of getting the result you want.

● *Don't get emotional.* However strongly you feel about the issue under discussion, don't allow yourself to become emotional about it. People see emotion and reason as opposites, and the more emotion you display, the less rational you will appear. You want to look like someone whose judgements and opinions are based on logical reasoning. Displays of emotion – especially negative emotions such as fear, anger, sadness and so on – will undermine your credibility and therefore your argument.

Fools rush in

If there's a round-robin discussion in which everyone takes it in turn to express their view, try to be as close to being the last to speak as you can. It gives you a chance to gauge the mood of the meeting, to collect extra facts and data as they are divulged, and to hear the main arguments that you will want to add to or refute. Be brief and succinct and, as the last to speak, yours will be the argument that sticks most firmly in many people's minds.

● *Praise other people's contributions.* You are far more likely to get the result you want from the meeting if you remain pleasant and popular with everyone. If people take against you for being aggressive, pompous, arrogant, sarcastic, belligerent or anything else, they will be far more reluctant to vote in your favour. So remain friendly, no matter what.

You are far more likely to get the result you want from the meeting if you remain pleasant and popular with everyone.

One of the best techniques for staying in favour is to praise other people and their contributions to the meeting. And especially, praise them when you are going on to disagree with them. For example, 'Monica is absolutely right to say that employee response is terribly important, and I was impressed that she managed to find so many relevant figures. But I think we have to take into account that many of our staff have only the haziest idea of what is really being proposed . . . ', and so on.

This technique makes you sound magnanimous and ready to acknowledge a good contribution – so when you subsequently disagree it clearly isn't personal prejudice or sour grapes. The conclusion everyone will have to draw is that your disagreement is based on sound and rational judgement. And the person with whom you have disagreed will take it far less personally if they feel they have also been praised publicly in the process.

Just one word of warning: if you disagree with people a lot, use this technique sparingly or very subtly. If people see it as a ruse rather than as a genuine expression of praise, it will sound very hollow. As a rule of thumb, the more genuine you are in your praise, the more genuine it will sound (no surprises there, but worth bearing in mind).

And what if you still lose?

There will always be times when you don't get the result you want. Even if your case was brilliant, there may be other factors. Office politics and personal prejudices can prevent the best argument from winning at times. So don't take it personally. Handle it with dignity and good grace, but get your disagreement minuted. It means when it all falls apart later – just as you predicted it would – you can remind the meeting that you disagreed with the decision all along. You won't be popular if you smugly gloat 'Told you so!', but a polite reference to your disagreement will remind people that your judgement was sound.

There will always be times when you don't get the result you want.

So if the decision goes against you, don't sulk or get upset or angry. Accept it. Say, 'If that's the feeling of the meeting, obviously I'll go along with it. But I still feel we'll encounter problems with low productivity and high costs. I'd be grateful, chairman, if my views could be minuted.' Simple, brief and amicable, but firm about your disagreement.

However, if you follow all the guidelines in this chapter for getting what you want out of meetings, you'll rarely find yourself in this position.

Summary

Before a meeting, you can give yourself the best chance of getting the outcome you want if you:

- talk to people; and
- prepare your case.

Once you're in the meeting, you need to put your case across strongly and convincingly.

- Be clear and succinct.
- Structure a cohesive argument: position, problem, possibilities, proposal.
- Don't get emotional.
- Praise other people's contributions.

CHAPTER EIGHT

Cope with stress

Stress can be one of the most debilitating conditions to have to cope with. It can cause anything from minor frustrations and demotivation through to serious or even fatal illness. Often it starts in a small way and then builds up, sometimes to the point where your work, your home life and your health all suffer significantly. So the sooner you tackle stress at work, the better.

Stress can be one of the most debilitating conditions to have to cope with.

If you identify the things that stress you most at work, you can consciously take action to minimize them. All jobs entail stress, and some entail a good deal, but you still want to reduce the stress as far as possible. I'm not talking here about positive pressure: many of us choose the jobs we do because we thoroughly enjoy working under stringent and challenging pressure, and are more stressed by boredom than by a tough deadline. Pressure becomes stress when it stops being fun and starts to generate negative emotions such as worry, frustration or anger.

Simply working out what it is that stresses you can often be a big part of the problem. Is it certain types of task? Is it the balance between home and work? Is it certain people who cause you problems? Simply identifying the problem often gives you the focus you need to tackle and resolve it.

Here's a list of typical stress factors you may encounter at work:

- time pressure
- difficult problems
- difficult people (boss included)
- poor communication
- pressure from the boss

- noise
- lack of recognition
- failure
- working alone
- negativity from boss and colleagues.

Talking to your boss can help with many stresses you can't control yourself. Your boss cannot control every factor which stresses you, but they do have at least some power over many of them. Again, once you have identified these you can do something about them, for example:

- Talk to your boss and explain the problem.
- Find your own ways to alleviate the stress.
- Find ways to deal with the stress, such as going for a run at lunchtime, talking it through with a friend, or even writing *I hate my boss* 20 times on a piece of paper (but don't ever let them find it).

Interruptions

In most offices, interruptions are a big problem. They add to stress simply because they waste your time. Even an important interruption, for something that really does need addressing, disturbs your train of thought and makes you less efficient. And time is at such a premium that lots of interruptions can mean going home later, becoming more tired, missing out home and social life and so on.

In most offices, interruptions are a big problem.

It is infuriating if you're concentrating hard on something, in the middle of a train of thought, and someone ambles in and starts talking about something that could easily have waited. Or perhaps they interrupt you just as havoc has broken out and you're frantically trying to meet a deadline that's just been pushed forward. How do you deal with it? Here are some techniques to use.

- At the risk of sounding obvious, one of the most effective techniques is to say, as they appear in the doorway, 'I'm very busy at the moment. Can this wait? I'll let you know as soon as I'm finished.'

- Aim to visit people in their office rather than have them visit you. It's much easier to time the visit to suit you – even if it only gives you time to get to a good stopping point in the next couple of minutes – and you can keep the interruption much shorter. Once they have their feet under your desk it may be hard to shift them. Obviously you can't predict a lot of interruptions, but you can predict a fair proportion of them. Maybe you know a colleague is planning to speak to you sometime today about the agenda for next Monday's meeting. In that case, visit them before they visit you. Or perhaps they call you up and say, 'Got a few minutes? Good. I'll just pop down the corridor and see you.' In this case, reply, 'Don't bother, I'll come and see you. I have to go that way anyway.'

- If you have a task lined up which requires your undiverted concentration, try to schedule it when you know the office will be quiet.

Do-as-you-would-be-done-by

Treat other people as you'd like them to treat you. It sends out a subliminal signal which won't cure a hardened interrupter on its own, but it will help to set an example. So don't interrupt other people if you can help it; save up several questions or points for a single interruption; and always ask if this is a good time before launching into your interruption. At the very least, it gives you the moral high ground. You're not expecting anything of them that you don't already do yourself.

- If you rarely shut the door to your office, simply doing so will send out a signal to everyone that you don't want to be disturbed.

- Divert your phone calls or switch on your voicemail to prevent people interrupting you by phone.

- If certain colleagues are frequently inclined to visit and outstay their welcome, get rid of any extra chairs in your office. Or cover them with files. If there's nowhere to sit and get comfortable, they'll leave much sooner.

- When someone interrupts you, be as brief as you can with them without being rude. If you sit and chat to them for ten minutes every time they

Deterrent techniques work best if you use them in moderation. interrupt, they can hardly be blamed for not realizing you needed to get on with your work. So be brisk and businesslike without being brusque, and they'll soon get the point. You can encourage people to leave simply by standing up.

Everything in moderation

All these deterrent techniques work best if you use them in moderation. If your door is always shut and your phone always diverted, people will have little choice but to interrupt if they want to speak to you. But if they know that you only use these techniques when you genuinely need to, they are far more likely to respect them.

Work overload

Your in-tray is the height of a small tower block, you can't find your phone under the pile of to-do lists and Post-it notes, your boss wants to see you in five minutes, you're due at a vital meeting in a quarter of an hour, and reception has just called to tell you there is a visitor to see you now.

Familiar? There's plenty of advice around (much of it plain unrealistic) on how to make sure you never build up a backlog, but it's too late for all that. (You'll find realistic help on working more effectively in Chapter 10.) You've *got* the backlog now, and the only question you need answered is, 'How do I get rid of it?'

Well, there are just six simple steps you need to follow to clear the work overload fast, so here they are.

1 You'll have to start by creating the time to deal with the pile-up.

- Tell yourself that an essential presentation to a key client or to the board of directors has just been scheduled for all day tomorrow. Can you make it? Great. Now here's some good news. It's just been cancelled. So you can use the whole day that you just freed up to clear your work backlog instead.

- If you absolutely cannot free up this much time at once, how about starting work an hour early each day for a week? This would buy you five hours before anyone else has arrived in the office to pester you. Be strict about forbidding yourself to do anything else in these five hours other than clear the pile-up of work.

2 The next stage is to identify your overall objective in your job; this means you can tackle the work in the most effective and productive order.

Identifying your objective doesn't have to take long – five minutes at the most and probably less. But the whole process of clearing the work over-load will be much faster in the long run if you just give this the time it needs.

If you're not entirely clear what your objective should be, try asking yourself this question: when you move on from this job, what single aspect of your company's performance should you hope to leave better than you found it? Customer satisfaction? Sales figures? Productivity? Costs? Public awareness? The answer to this will tell you what your objective is.

3 After this, you can sort all the hundreds (or even thousands) of individual tasks into just a few key groups.

The precise groups you choose to sort things into will be determined by your particular job. But we're looking at categories like:

- phone calls
- data for Monday's meeting
- filing
- reading material
- stuff to pass on to other people
- Project A
- Project B (and so on).

You can put your rubbish straight in the bin if you like. But if there's a lot of it, you may find it hugely encouraging to keep a pile for it so that you can see how much progress you're making. This is just the sort of positive boost which can make the whole operation more satisfying. And that, in turn, can help you to work through it faster.

4 The next step involves measuring these groups against your objective so that you can prioritize.

The closer a particular category is to meeting your objective, the higher you should prioritize it. So if Project A is all about increasing your customer base, and that's your real objective in this job, Project A is top priority. If all your reading material is administrative and won't further your objective, it gets a low priority.

It is very tempting to move the tasks you enjoy up your list, and put the tasks you don't want to do at the bottom of the list. Don't do it. Be brutally objective about ranking tasks, or you will end up back where you started before you know it – with unimportant jobs done and a pile of tasks on your desk which are urgent and important and should have been done already. You've got to deal with it all sooner or later, so when it comes to your least favourite tasks, just bite the bullet.

Why not use three different colours of files for all your work, coded according to importance? This means you are constantly reminding yourself of where your priorities really lie, and it saves a lot of time whenever you come to prioritize your workload (even when it isn't piling up).

5 Now you come to dealing with the actual tasks themselves, and the options for doing this – do it, defer it, delegate it or dump it.

Be brutally objective about ranking tasks, or you will end up back where you started before you know it.

Don't be tempted to address the most important tasks now simply because they are important. If they are not urgent, they can still be deferred. It will give you more time to do them justice. Dump everything which you can get away with not doing.

Drawing up schedules may not seem like a clever use of time, but it's just what you need to do now. You are doubtless itching to get on with all those piles of tasks by now. But it is the only way to make sure you don't reach the end of your time before you reach the end of the workload. So allocate your time for dealing with the remaining tasks. One of the first things we tend to do when we are rushing is to stop thinking. But by thinking *smart* – setting an objective, drawing up a schedule and so on – we are investing a few minutes now to save a load of time later. Trust me.

6   Finally, you need to ensure that the tasks you deal with yourself take up as little time as possible.

Making responses to people can sometimes be staved off if you're pushed for time by simply acknowledging their call, letter or e-mail. Send them a note or an e-mail which says, 'Thanks for your letter/e-mail/call. I am giving it some thought and will get back to you in the next few days.' Make sure you do so, of course, but you've bought yourself two or three days' grace.

Do it, defer it, delegate it or dump it.

Sometimes you need to call someone who you know is likely to trap you on the phone. If you are one of those people who is under-assertive about extricating yourself, call when you're pretty sure they will be out and leave a voicemail message instead.

Once you've cleared the backlog of work, you should find your stress levels easing miraculously. Follow the advice on easing interruptions, and look at Chapter 10 to find out how to prevent the backlog building up again, and you'll be on course for a far more stress-free working life.

Nerves

Almost all of us feel nervous before an important presentation, meeting or interview. After all, it's something that matters to us that we need to get right. So nerves are only natural. But of course there's a world of difference between a little shot of adrenalin that keeps you on your toes, and a paralyzing numbness that dries your mouth out, makes you sweat copiously, and renders you incapable of speech.

Nerves are only natural.

In fact, most of us fall between these two extremes. But if you're one of the people who finds that nerves get in the way, what can you do about it? Well, you'll be pleased to know that almost all cases of severe nerves can be reduced to a manageable level, and the less severe cases can all but disappear. It just takes preparation.

Root of the problem

The key lies in understanding what causes an attack of nerves. And the root cause is fear. Fear of what could go wrong, from drying up completely to making a fool of yourself by spilling your coffee. The more remote these failures and catastrophes seem, the more remote will be your fears. This is why you often notice a couple of minutes into a nerve-wracking experience that you're not nearly as nervous as you were just before you began: things are going fine, you realize you're not making a prat of yourself and you are able to speak normally after all.

Worst case

What do you do if something really goes catastrophically wrong? You spill water all down yourself, or knock a huge pile of papers across the floor. Or maybe you're so nervous you can't remember the name of the person you're talking to. It's not likely to happen after you've read this chapter, but just supposing . . .

The answer is to laugh at yourself, and admit to being nervous. Say something like, 'That's what nerves can do to you! It shows how important this is to me.' There's no reason why your boss, customer or whoever you're dealing with should count it against you, so long as you show you can respond well and with humour.

If you can minimize the likelihood of things going wrong, you will minimize your fears. Of course there will still be a small, irrational panic at the very back of your mind, at least until the session is under way, but it need cause no more than a touch of adrenalin which simply keeps you thinking fast.

Your best bet is to rehearse as thoroughly as you can.

- For an interview, think through your replies to likely questions and tough ones, and practise your answers in front of a mirror. Rehearse your opening greeting. Try on your outfit in advance if you haven't worn it recently.

- If you're nervous about an important meeting, think of ways to express the key points you want to make succinctly, or persuasive ways to rebut counter-arguments you expect to encounter. Rehearse these thoroughly.

- For a presentation, prepare thoroughly in advance and then rehearse, rehearse, rehearse. Rehearse in front of a mirror, and practise with any props or visual aids until you know exactly how to handle them.

Last-minute check

Five minutes before your interview, meeting or presentation, nip into the cloakroom and do a quick check in the mirror – teeth, hair, tie, earrings, buttons, zips. Then you won't have to worry about them when you get there.

But you will still want to take other precautions. Your motto should be: be prepared. Anticipate disaster, consider every possible emergency or embarrassment you can, and plan for it. That way, it won't happen or – even if it does – you'll be ready to cope. Here are some antidotes to one or two classic adrenalin-starters.

Adrenalin-starter	Antidote
Coffee and tea	If you're worried you'll spill your drink, simply decline when offered. In fact, caffeine's not a great idea anyway if you're nervous – avoid it for the previous couple of hours too (along with any form of alcohol).
Looking nervous	Actually, no one cares if you look nervous so long as you still do the job well. But we often fear appearing to be nervous. If you are inclined to shake at the beginning, fold your hands together in front of you, or in your lap, where they can keep each other under control.

Mouth turning dry	When you turn down the coffee, ask for a glass of water instead. If you don't need it, it's OK to leave it (you don't have to drink it and have the worry of spilling it).
Unable to think of anything to say	Here's another time the glass of water comes in handy. Taking a sip or two before you respond to a tricky question buys you a few moments to get your head straight.
Difficult questions	Get someone to role play a question and answer session with you and brief them to be as difficult as possible. That way, the real thing will be a breeze by comparison.

Easing the symptoms

As far as coping with the physical symptoms of nerves is concerned, try to eat beforehand. Don't binge, but a light breakfast or lunch will help (unless you honestly think you'll bring it straight back up). Nerves are always worse on an empty stomach.

The way to reduce stress is to relax, and slow breathing is a quick-fix for this.

You may also find relaxation exercises helpful. The way to reduce stress is to relax, and slow breathing is a quick-fix for this. Here's an exercise which you can do moments before your presentation, meeting or interview, for example, while you're waiting at reception or in a nearby office.

Relaxation exercise

1 Sit down if possible, but you can do this standing up if necessary.
2 Relax your arms and hands. If you're sitting down, put your hands in your lap.
3 Close your eyes if you can, but again this isn't essential.

4 Breathe in through your nose, slowly, to a count of five. Breathe in as low down as you can, pushing out your diaphragm and stomach.

5 Breathe out through your mouth to a count of seven. If you are sitting down, don't slump as you breathe out.

6 Allow your breathing to return to normal and open your eyes.

You can repeat this at intervals as often as you need to, but always let your breathing return to normal in between. If you don't, you may hyperventilate. This won't do you any harm, but it can make you feel a little light-headed which may make you more nervous rather than more relaxed.

Even once the session is under way, there are still techniques you can use on the spot to help you relax.

- Take a deep breath whenever you get a chance to stop speaking. The more tense we get, the more our ribs and chest lock up. By releasing them with a deep, chest-expanding breath, you ease the tension so it can't build up. This requires no concentration, so you can still focus on what you should be thinking about.

- Smiling helps to relax your muscles. You may feel like an idiot if you grin inanely all the time, but if you can find opportunities to smile it will relax you. And it will help you come across as a warm and friendly person, too.

- If you notice yourself sitting hunched up, legs and arms crossed (not to mention fingers), shift to a more open and relaxed position. The important thing for relaxation is just to open up and allow your muscles to relax. Your muscles may tense up as a result of psychological nervousness, but you can reverse the cause and effect: relaxing your muscles can make you feel less nervous.

Summary

To minimize interruptions:

- Discourage people from visiting your office, or from staying long if they do visit.
- Use your voicemail.

- Schedule high-concentration tasks at realistic times when interruptions are least likely.

- Shut your door occasionally to signify that you don't want to be disturbed.

- Always be polite but brief, so people get into the habit of interrupting you quickly rather than staying to chat.

To manage a work overload:

- Create some time to tackle the problem.

- Identify your overall objective.

- Sort the tasks into a few key groups.

- Prioritize these groups by assessing them against your objective.

- Deal with each task in one of four ways: do it, defer it, delegate it or dump it.

- Get through the remaining tasks as swiftly as you can.

To reduce nerves:

Prepare yourself as much as you can for the meeting, presentation or interview. The more you have rehearsed and prepared, the less you have to fear. And the less you have to fear, the less nervous you will feel.

- Practise your responses.

- Plan to avoid or cope with the biggest adrenalin-starters.

- Use simple relaxation techniques to ease nerves on the day.

CHAPTER NINE

Improve your personal profile

Who do you reckon are the high fliers among your colleagues? If you were in charge, who would you be giving the pay rises and promotions to? Some people just stand out as being valuable employees before you've even considered their specific skills or the wealth they generate for the organization. It's worth thinking about what gives someone an air of success, because once you know what the ingredients are, you can begin to cultivate them for yourself.

Your personal image

The way you come across to other people is an important part of how they assess your value. So it's well worth sprucing up your personal image to let your boss and more senior management see that you are an asset to the organization. This isn't a matter of trying to turn yourself into someone else – that never works – it's just a case of building on key strengths and minimizing weaknesses.

The way you come across to other people is an important part of how they assess your value.

The list below covers the key characteristics which will give you an image of success. The vast majority of us possess many of these already, but we have some areas where there is room for improvement. That's what this is about: making a conscious effort to project the best possible side of ourselves at all times.

Don't expect miracles here. It will take people a while to notice the change, but they will notice it eventually. I have a friend I've known for about 20 years. He was always thoroughly unreliable, arriving ludicrously late – if at all – when invited for a meal or a party. Not long ago I made an arrangement with him and then teased him saying, 'I don't know why I bother inviting you for a particular time, it won't make any difference.' He then pointed out to me that he had made a deliberate decision about three years earlier to arrive on time and be generally more reliable. Thinking back, I realized for the first time that he had, in fact, been consistently on time for the last few years, and always phoned if he was delayed or couldn't make it. But I'd never noticed the improvement. Now, however, my opinion of his reliability has changed.

If you improve on aspects of your personal image, it may not be noticed right away. But if your boss comments that you often display a negative attitude, for example, you can point out that they'll be hard pressed to quote a recent example of your negativity because you have been consciously adopting a more positive approach. And, of course, newcomers to the organization (including new managers more senior than you) will see only your new, positive image and take it for granted.

No Superman

Your mission is not to transform yourself, like Clark Kent, into someone unrecognizable. Simply make the decision to work on those areas where you can improve your image and become someone whom everyone sees as a high flier.

Personal appearance

One of the keys to improving your image is to be consistent. If you look smart four days a week but always come in rumpled and over-casual on a Monday morning, at the start of each week you are undoing the good work of every Tuesday-through-Friday. If your company's dress code is informal, that's fine. But make sure your clothes are clean and pressed every day – not just the days you have important meetings. And dress appropriately for the job in terms of accessories, jewellery and so on, as well as clothes. Your hair, teeth and nails should always be clean, and if smoking isn't part of the corporate culture, keep any evidence of it well concealed.

Energy

You must have noticed how some people come across as being limp and mousey, or half-asleep, even though in some cases you know they are very productive workers. Others have a sense of energy and dynamism about them which is invigorating and inspiring to be around. They are the ones who appear successful, even if they're not especially so. When they really *are* good performers too, they are the ones who seem to win all the prizes and get what they want every time.

> **We can't all have the charisma of a film star, but we can all inject more energy into our behaviour.**

Wouldn't it be nice to be one of them? Well, you can. We can't all have the charisma of a film star, but we can all inject more energy into our behaviour, and that's the key to appearing dynamic and capable of high achievement. Here are some simple techniques for boosting your image. You'll be doing some of them already – just add the rest to your repertoire, and get into the habit of projecting energy *all* the time, instead of just on good days.

- Speak clearly and don't mumble.
- When you meet people, smile and be ready with a firm handshake.
- Make eye contact regularly when you talk to people.
- Say hello promptly and with enthusiasm (practise all these in front of a mirror until they come naturally).
- Don't always wait for the other person to speak – be the first to initiate a conversation at least half the time.
- Sound interested in what you are saying and in what others have to say to you.
- Move and speak at an upbeat (but not rushed) pace.

There. That wasn't difficult, was it? But it will make a big difference to your personal image.

Positive attitude

If you're a natural optimist, you won't have a problem in this department. But if you're a pessimist (OK, OK, sorry, I meant a realist), you may find it tougher. The thing is, most people get depressed when they are exposed to negative comments. They find people who always look on the downside of every issue (as they see it) irritating and frustrating.

Silver lining

Make it a rule that you won't ever bring a problem to someone unless you have a solution to offer, too. It may not be the best solution, but at least it gets you out of difficulty. So don't say to your boss, 'The new brochures for the trade show haven't turned up and the lorry's leaving to set up the stand in an hour. What do we do?' It's far better to say, 'The new brochures for the trade show haven't turned up, but I figured you might be able to take them when you come up on Friday morning. Or we could courier them – it's expensive but they're important, so it would be worth it. What do you think?' Now doesn't that sound better? That's the kind of person your boss wants to work with.

Having said that, realists are important people to have around. They keep everyone else's feet on the ground, and ensure that potential problems are identified well in advance. If this is you, you're doing an important job; don't stop. It's just a matter of presentation. Carry on pointing out problems, but find a way of expressing them that sounds more acceptable to all those optimists you work with (sorry, I mean woolly-headed idealists).

There's a three-step process to making your realistic comments sound positive rather than negative to everyone else, described below.

1   First, make all your negative comments specific, because that makes them useful. Instead of saying, 'It'll never work' (a singularly unhelpful comment), say, 'It'll never work because the costs are too high.'

2   Next, never express a negative view without a positive one attached to it. So instead of saying, 'It'll never work because the costs are too high', say, 'It would certainly increase throughput, but it'll never work because the costs are too high.'

3   Finally, tone down your language so that you talk about 'worries' and 'concerns', for example, rather than insisting that things are 'wrong' or 'major problems'. So you might say, 'It would certainly increase throughput. My one concern is that it's going to be hard to get the costs low enough to make it work.'

You've made exactly the same point you always intended to but now, all of a sudden, instead of coming across as negative, you appear helpful and constructive. And you've made a valuable contribution by pointing out where the proposal still needs work. And all you changed was the way you presented your view.

Likeableness

Popular people do better at work and are more likely to get what they want. They are more fun to have around, generate a positive atmosphere and improve morale. And as a colleague being asked to co-operate, a customer negotiating a deal or a manager being asked for a pay rise, wouldn't you be more sympathetic towards someone you liked? So if you're less popular than you could be, take a look through this list of likeable behaviour and see where there's room for improvement.

> **Popular people do better at work and are more likely to get what they want.**

- Be a good listener.
- Show an interest in the people around you.
- Don't be arrogant or pompous.
- Don't gossip about people behind their backs.
- Never put people down.

- A strong sense of humour is a definite plus, but don't use it against the people you work with.

- If you manage your own team, be fair and always make time when your team members need to talk to you.

None of this is difficult, but most of us know deep down that we don't really listen properly, or that when we disagree with someone's idea, we sometimes put them down ('That's a stupid idea!', rather than, 'I disagree').

Trust and reliability

You are bound to succeed better if you are regarded as being trustworthy and reliable. So make sure you never break confidences or act disloyally, for example by gossiping about colleagues to customers or suppliers. Equally, always show you can be trusted to get tasks done, especially when they are urgent or important. Show that even when delays have put you behind, you can still get the work done without mistakes. That means that when there's a sense of panic, your boss will decide to put *you* in charge of vital projects – you can be trusted to make sure it all runs smoothly. That'll give you a few feathers in your cap when you come to ask for whatever it is you want from your boss.

Open up

People who are open and honest tend to be seen as more trustworthy than those who are private or secretive. It's not really fair most of the time, but that's the way it is. If you are a private person, try to be a little more forthcoming about yourself – you'll find it helps your image. You don't have to bare your soul; just join in talking about your holiday or discussing your favourite music, or tell the odd anecdote about when you were a child.

Visibility

It's important to improve your personal profile in the ways we've just looked at, but all of this may be of no use if you don't get yourself noticed. If all the perks or rewards you want are going to be at the sole discretion of your immediate boss, this may not be an issue. But if decisions are taken, or have to be approved, further up the organization, you need to be sure that you get noticed in the right quarters. When your boss breaks it to their boss that you're asking for a pay rise, for example, you don't want the response to be, 'Who?'

All the techniques we've just covered – having energy, being likeable and confident and so on – will be a big help. But you want something more. You want your name, your face and your success to stand out from the crowd. Here are a few ideas which will help.

- Make sure everyone knows you. Network within your company and forge as many links as possible with other departments – all ones which put you in a positive light, of course. So whenever accounts need someone to dig up some information for them, production want a trainer to run a course for them, or marketing need extra bodies to run an exhibition stand, make sure you volunteer. You'll meet other managers as well as your own, and become one of those people everyone knows.

Make sure everyone knows you. Network within your company and forge as many links as possible with other departments.

- Look for the high profile tasks to volunteer for. If your boss is looking for someone to put together a report for senior management, make sure you offer to do it. If there's a presentation to the board coming up, offer to help. You may even be able to bring your experience to other departments – see if you can't get involved with an important project by offering to handle the press side of it, or put together a computer program for them, or whatever it is you're particularly skilled at.

- Whenever you do come face to face with senior management, follow the guidelines earlier in this chapter to make sure you give a good impression and don't simply merge into the background. In particular, speak occasionally but not too often. At meetings or events we all tend to make about one really smart comment for every few ordinary ones (and the occasional really stupid remark we can't quite believe we said). We have one great idea for each half-dozen mediocre ones. Well, when you're around top management, don't open your mouth until you've come up with the really smart idea. That way you'll earn an enviable reputation as someone who doesn't talk too much, but everything you do say is really worth listening to.

Earn an enviable reputation as someone who doesn't talk too much, but everything you do say is really worth listening to.

It's not enough to be valuable. You have to be seen to be valuable. So make sure not only your boss but everyone else too is fully aware what an asset you are to the department and to the organization. Make it an ongoing policy to have a positive and high profile all the time.

Summary

To get what you want at work, you need a strong and impressive personal profile. This doesn't mean changing your personality, but simply capitalizing on your strengths and minimizing your weaker points. If people both like you and are impressed by your working style, they are far more likely to give you what you want. The key areas you need to work on are:

- personal image
- likeableness
- visibility.

CHAPTER TEN

Work effectively

Let's try a simple test. Here are some characteristics of two people; let's suppose they are colleagues of yours. All you have to do is decide which of these two people you think is the more productive worker.

Person A	Person B
• Always arrives on time to meetings and appointments	• Frequently late for meetings and appointments
• Always has the necessary papers, diary or whatever with them	• Often arrives without the necessary paperwork
• Always remembers to make phone calls when agreed	• Forgets to make promised call backs
• Chases up suppliers, colleagues and so on when they forget to follow up arrangements	• Frequently complains of being let down by suppliers, colleagues and so on failing to fulfil arrangements and promises

That wasn't difficult, was it? Clearly person A is more productive, and person A is more likely to get what they want than person B for two reasons:

1 Because they work more effectively.

2 Because they *look as if* they work more effectively.

In other words, not only are their results going to be better than they otherwise would, but the boss is going to perceive them as an effective worker. Actually, person A may not perform as well as person B because they lack the ability, but they'll still look better. So if you're one of those people who claim that you work better surrounded by mess, I don't care. Even if it's true, it won't help you. Your boss will see you as disorganized whatever the truth is, and your chances of getting what you want will be damaged.

If you are already neurotically tidy and well organized, congratulations. You can skip on to the next chapter. But if you think there is any room for improvement in this area, read on. You need to improve your image as an effective person, as well as making your work style genuinely more stream-lined.

Now, if you're not naturally disorganized, the idea of turning into a paragon of organization is unthinkable. There are all sorts of reasons you can come up with against it. Let me guess:

- You're naturally disorganized and a leopard can't change its spots.
- It takes time to get organized and you haven't got that sort of time.
- Naturally organized people are all neurotic and uptight and you'd rather lose your job than turn into one of them.

No doubt you've got plenty more where those came from. Well, let's get something straight. No one is trying to turn you into something you're not. You can go on being a disorganized person, so long as **You can go on being a disorganized person, so long as you just adopt a few organized behaviours.** you just adopt a few organized behaviours. What you do when your bosses aren't looking is up to you, but if you want to be a success at work, you'll have to make just a small effort to get into a few new habits. That's all. And once they have become habits, you won't even notice you're doing them. OK?

Finding time

This is the *only* difficult bit, and anyone good enough to deserve to get what they want has got to be capable of managing time once they know how.

Organized people don't manage their lives by instinct, you know. They have lists and notes to make it all possible. The only difference between you and them is that they write things down which you wouldn't get round to writing down. That's it.

It's a small difference, but it has a huge impact. It makes them effective workers, so their productivity improves. Tasks get done in good time instead of being left to the last minute, and they have enough time for the crucial job of planning and working towards major objectives, instead of always running to keep still on routine tasks with no time for the big, important stuff like generating profitable and productive ideas.

Pep talk

If you dread having to make yourself find extra time, just give yourself a good talking to. If you are capable enough to deserve success, you're capable enough to find just a few minutes a day to organize your life. If you have ever managed to diet, give up smoking or keep a New Year resolution, you have what it takes to do this.

If you could simply find ten to twenty minutes a day to do all that writing down, you could reap all those benefits too. There. That's the only tough bit – making yourself set aside those few minutes each day to do all the planning that will make you organized and effective. So when will you do it?

- You can arrive at work early and use the quiet time before everyone else turns up – so long as you know you can avoid other distractions.
- You could schedule time in your diary, so long as you don't allow it to be pushed aside for anything else.
- You could have a rule that you do it at the end of the day, and you don't allow yourself to leave the office until you've done it.
- Maybe you could find a regular time each day on the train to or from work.
- You could even do it at home in the evening, so long as it fits round the rest of your personal life.

The rules here should be obvious: choose your time but make sure you do it religiously, every day. Pick a regular time which works for you (regular so it becomes a habit) and *never* allow it to be edged out by other things. Once you start to fall behind, you're on a slippery slope. This is inevitably the biggest danger for naturally disorganized people. But organize only these few minutes each day and everything else will fall into place. I promise. If you don't believe me, just try it for a fortnight. Once it has become a habit to spend this time, you'll find it becomes as easy as finding time for other habits such as taking a morning shower or eating lunch. What's more, this time is an investment. Once you're into the swing of the new system you'll find it generates far more time than it occupies.

Organizing your working life

Right. So that's sorted. You've cleared about a quarter of an hour a day to get organized, so what are you going to do with it? Before I answer that question, I have a confession to make. I lied. Clearing this time isn't the only thing you have to do. But it is the only difficult thing – honest.

Get yourself a notebook and a pen and never let them out of your sight.

The other thing you have to do is really easy. You have to get yourself a notebook and a pen and never let them out of your sight. Organizing is a two-part operation: you spend the day intelligence-gathering, and then you sit down for your 15-minute stint to collate all the information you've assembled. During the day, write down everything that comes along which will have any impact at all in the future, whether that's tomorrow or next year. You should jot down the following:

- Every time you promise to make a phone call later in the week ('I'll call you Friday afternoon').

- Every time anyone says they'll contact you ('I'll get back to you when I've put together a quote').

- Every meeting, appointment or event that gets mentioned which you need to know about – even if you don't actually have to be there ('We'll be discussing that point at next Tuesday's departmental meeting').

- Every point for action that you think of or anyone mentions ('I must go and take a look at the new store once it's open').

Jot them down as scrappily as you like, in any kind of shorthand, so long as you can read it back later. If someone gives you a memo, minutes of a meeting, a brochure, an e-mail, a Post-it note or anything else which contains information about dates, times or action points, keep them in a folder rather than bothering to copy them across to your notebook (which obviously just wouldn't get done).

See? This bit really isn't difficult. Each note you jot down takes only a moment, and within a couple of days you'll be so into the habit of it that you won't even notice you're doing it. And you should find that it gives you a wonderful sense of control. Everything you need is in that notebook – you're completely on top of the workload. There is just one vital rule: *never go anywhere without the notebook*. You must have all your information in one place (or all put instantly into the single folder you also keep for the purpose). If you start leaving notes dotted around the place, you're back in the land of disorder, and the process will stop being easy.

Little and often

There is a simple rule to keeping organized: little and often. Whether it is a matter of keeping the diary up to date, tidying your desk, getting the filing done or working through phone calls, the trick is to catch up frequently so that the workload in question never gets out of hand. You'll hardly notice the time it takes to file two or three items a day, but if you leave it for as little as a fortnight you might have dozens of items in a pile you simply can't face tackling. Try to get into the habit of dealing with these kinds of tasks as they arise so you never get that sinking feeling.

The diary

So now you're ready to sit down for 15 minutes at the beginning or end of each day. And you are going to transfer the variety of notes in your notebook across to your diary. All of them. For this, you need a decent-sized diary. Go and get one if necessary. You need one which has room for notes, as well as having each day broken down by times.

The core of getting organized, working productively and looking effective is a well-planned diary. Boy, does that sound boring – the sort of thing a Monty Python-style accountant would have. But actually it's not so bad. In fact the feeling of control it gives you is rather enjoyable. And your ten to twenty minutes a day is there to keep your diary (or should I say your bible?) in order.

> **The core of getting organized, working productively and looking effective is a well-planned diary.**

As well as your 15 minutes each day, you will also need to find a few extra minutes at the start of each month for diary planning. In fact, you need to schedule four stages of planning, all very simple:

- yearly
- monthly
- weekly
- daily.

Yearly planning

At the start of each year, you'll need to spend about half an hour (which you will have scheduled into your diary for the purpose) entering all the dates of which you already have details for the rest of the year, such as:

- regular meetings
- special events (trade shows or product launches, for example)
- regular events (a monthly departmental lunch, or a weekly team meeting)
- holidays
- personal time (if you want to plan a day off for the kids' birthdays or leave early on the evening of an anniversary).

You should also schedule:

- fifteen minutes at the start of each month for a similar diary session
- at least one full day a month – more if possible – for working on major pro-active tasks such as developing ideas and planning productive new projects.

Monthly planning

Repeat this on a smaller scale at the beginning of each month. Schedule time for things you didn't plan at the start of the year. This is especially important for managers, who need to schedule:

- selection interviews
- appraisals
- presentations (including preparation time)
- time to prepare reports and proposals
- time to delegate key tasks.

If your month is already looking overly full (and you know how many unplanned things tend to crop up, so be realistic), now is the time to trim your workload if you need to. Cancel or excuse yourself from meetings you don't really need to hold or attend, delegate anything you can, and stream-line your diary. For example, if you have two trips to the north west planned this month, move them both to the same day.

Two by two

Always look for opportunities to do two tasks at once if you can still give each the attention it needs. For example, do your filing (which you never allow to build up, of course) while you are holding for people on the phone. Or begin entering your notes into your diary while you're waiting for a meeting to get started, to save time later.

Weekly planning

Once you're into the swing, this takes only five minutes on a Monday morning (or the previous Friday evening if you prefer). Start filling in some of the blank spaces in your diary by scheduling time for:

- Delegation.
- Monitoring any staff who work for you.
- Catching up with phone calls.
- Dealing with miscellaneous tasks (these are the ones which really mess up your diary system if you haven't scheduled them – they push in and throw everything else out). Friday afternoons are a good time to block in an hour or two for this.
- Taking phone calls – then get the receptionist or an assistant to field calls saying you'll definitely be available on Wednesday afternoon, for example, or before 10.30 on Friday.

Daily planning

This is your ten-to-twenty-minute session that you are going to get into the habit of holding each day. Write down on the relevant page in your diary everything you have gleaned from your intelligence-gathering operations during the day.

- If you noted down that you would phone someone on Monday morning, enter it in the diary for Monday morning (with a brief note to remind you why you're calling).
- If you were handed a leaflet for an event you need to attend, which you stored in your folder, transfer the date to your diary (along with any contact phone number).
- If someone promised to call you back on Tuesday, make a note for Tuesday to prompt them. If they didn't give you a specific date by when they would contact you, write the reminder for whichever day you would expect them to have replied by.
- If you made an action point to write a letter, note it down for a time when you are scheduled to write letters, or to do miscellaneous tasks.

- Add into the diary any meetings, appointments or other dates and times you have collected during the day, and any contact names, phone numbers or directions for getting there which you might conceivably need.

The more organized your diary, the less you need to prioritize – it only arises when you don't have time for everything.

By doing this, you will find that when you open your diary each morning, it will already include a list of phone calls to make and things to do, all entered over the last few days and weeks. If you find that you need time scheduled in to work through these, simply make sure you give yourself a regular time. For example, you might arrive at 9.00 each morning, but ensure you never make an appointment earlier than 9.30, so you have half an hour at the start of each day to keep on top of phone calls and daily action points.

Prioritize

Organized people have all sorts of systems and codes for prioritizing tasks. But the more organized your diary, the less you need to prioritize – it only arises when you don't have time for everything. However it is worth having some kind of code to indicate, as you make a note in your diary, whether it is urgent that you do it on the day it is entered (just in case an emergency crops up and things slip . . .). Pick whatever system suits you – underline it, write it in red ink, run a highlighter pen over it. It's up to you.

Summary

Having a well-organized diary means:

- Nothing gets forgotten.
- Action points – both yours and other people's – are followed up regularly so work doesn't need to fall behind.

- Tasks can be scheduled well ahead so there is no need to find yourself doing last-minute tasks (apart from genuinely unforeseeable ones). This is clearly more effective, and makes the whole atmosphere of work more relaxed.

- Everything is scheduled (or consciously abandoned if you can see there is no time for it), which means you never have to be late for anything. We are generally late because we've tried to slot in extra tasks, or find out too late that a task is taking longer than we thought.

- The important tasks such as project planning and planning to meet objectives are properly scheduled in so you actually have time to do them.

So keep a notebook with you all the time to make notes, along with a folder for storing memos, Post-its and the like. And spend about 15 minutes a day transferring these notes into your diary. You will need to have a brief diary session:

- yearly
- monthly
- weekly
- daily.

If you can just find a few minutes a day for this, you'll find that your working life is transformed. You will be organized, in control, on time . . . in short, the kind of effective and productive worker whom everyone can see thoroughly deserves to get what they want.

If you can just find a few minutes a day for planning, you'll find that your working life is transformed.

There are plenty of other tips and techniques around for managing your time more effectively – and plenty of good books and courses on the subject – but getting on top of your diary, with all the concomitant benefits it brings, is the single most effective way to look organized and work more productively.

11

Be creative

Some people are full of ideas. Don't you just envy them? They have neat ideas for making things run more smoothly, and big ideas that generate income or positive publicity or better productivity for the organization. They are known as 'ideas people', and they are the ones who get whatever they want. Everyone can see how valuable and deserving they are.

> **'Ideas people' are the ones who get whatever they want. Everyone can see how valuable and deserving they are.**

So *you'd* better be an ideas person too, then, hadn't you? Why should those creative colleagues have all the ideas and get all the rewards? You know, there's a popular myth that some people are born creative and the rest of us simply don't have that particular spark. Well, cobblers to that. Believe it or not, creativity is a skill you can learn like any other. And you'd better believe it, because it's a skill you'll need if you want to be a success.

The trick to having good ideas is simply to have lots of ideas. Creative geniuses such as Albert Einstein and the Nobel prize-winning chemist Linus Pauling have testified to the fact that the proportion of good ideas doesn't change much. Pauling said, 'The best way to get a good idea is to get lots of ideas.' If you have one good idea in every ten, you'll have ten in every hundred and so on. The skill of creativity lies simply in producing a high volume of ideas, and then sifting them to identify the winners among them.

Change the record

So you need lots of ideas, and some of them are bound to be good ones. But how do you do that? Well, you need to find a new way of thinking. Obvious, really. If your current way of thinking isn't generating ideas, clearly a change is called for. The thing is, the way we habitually think is great for applying ideas, for working logically through projects, for dealing with routine tasks. It works, so we go on using it.

But there are other ways of thinking which, although less effective for these tasks, are better for generating creative ideas and solutions. They don't work well for routine use (which is why highly creative people, locked into creative mode, often function poorly in the real world; look at Van Gogh or Mozart), but they are just what you need for occasional use when you want to be creative.

The skill of creativity entails learning how to think in a way which helps your mind to explore ideas and problems from new angles.

The trouble with the way we usually think is that it turns into a habit. Our minds are so used to following certain lines of thought that they no longer break away to adopt a more creative approach – unless we consciously tell them to. The skill of creativity entails learning how to think in a way which helps your mind to explore ideas and problems from new angles.

There has to be an answer

Much research has been done to indicate that one of the keys to finding a creative answer to a question is your own belief that there *is* an answer. If you set your creative mind a challenge, it is important that you believe it can be met. If you are confident that there is a solution, you are far more likely to reach it. As Henry Ford said, 'Whether you believe you can, or whether you believe you can't, you're absolutely right.'

Creativity is all about opening up new paths in your mind which you have previously not used. Don't allow your thinking to become stuck in a rut, but force it to adopt new methods. Set yourself a question – a problem to solve or new ideas to generate. For example:

- How can I spend my PR budget most effectively?
- What would resolve the bottleneck in production?
- How can Matt and I share a computer terminal without coming to blows?
- How can we boost productivity in this department?
- What would ease the current conflict over the holiday rota?
- What new products would most appeal to our customers?

Creativity is always linked to a particular challenge, so phrase your question clearly. That way, your creative mind will know precisely what you are asking of it.

The techniques

Now you're ready to be as creative a thinker as anyone else. You've decided what question to address your creative skills to, and you have simply to choose a new way of thinking about the question. There are dozens of techniques for creative thinking; here are a few of the quickest and most simple to use.

Problem reversal

This is a quick and easy creativity technique. All you have to do is to phrase your problem – for example, 'everyone wants to go on holiday at the same time' – and then reverse it. So you might get 'no one wants to go on holiday at all'. (If there's more than one way to reverse the phrase, it doesn't matter, so long as you generate a phrase which describes a broadly opposite problem.) Now try to think of solutions to this reversed problem. How about these?

- We close the business for a specified holiday so everyone goes on holiday at the same time.

- We pay people to go on holiday.
- We allocate holidays to people.

You might be wondering where this has got you. Well, it's opened up new channels of thinking, that's what. You can now look at these apparently barmy ideas and use them to generate new and feasible ideas to the real problem. For example:

- Closing down for a standard holiday period might lead you to think about whether it really matters if everyone wants their holiday at the same time. Maybe for the price of a temp or two, the department could work around a couple of weeks with almost no one in the office.

- Paying people to go on holiday sounds pretty daft. But what about offering some people a bonus if they agree to forego some of their holiday, or to take it at an unpopular time? It would ease the pressures of under-staffing.

- Allocating holidays from on high isn't likely to go down well. But perhaps those people who want to take holidays on oversubscribed dates could work out their own system of allocation. It can't be hard to persuade them that a solution needs to be found – either they find it themselves or it may have to be imposed on them. They can draw lots, or maybe have a rota system – if you choose first this summer you get last choice at Christmas.

The more you can relax, the better you free up your unconscious mind to generate creative ideas for you.

You see, this is a quick and simple technique for coming up with some original options. Everyone is different – you would probably have come up with different solutions from the same problem reversal. That's fine. So long as you generate original and realistic ideas, you can present creative solutions to your team – preferably a choice of creative solutions.

Stay cool

Although these techniques are effective whatever your mood, you will find that the more you can relax, the better you free up your unconscious mind to generate creative ideas for you. I know this isn't a great moment to say this if you have a crucial decision impending, but . . . try to relax.

Random stimulation

Like most creativity techniques, this one's fun too. And fast. The idea is really to knock your mind sideways into a different way of thinking – so you come up with different ideas from last time.

Start by selecting a word at random. Try opening a dictionary with your eyes shut, pointing at a word, and then opening your eyes. This is the word you have to work with. If you haven't got a dictionary to hand, pick the name of the first object you see, or take a random word from another book. Suppose you pick the word 'sugar'. Now think about sugar for a while.

- It's sweet.
- It comes from a plant.
- It comes in lumps or grains.
- You can eat it.
- There are lots of varieties.
- It makes you fat.

It's up to you what attributes of sugar you come up with. You don't have to be comprehensive. After thinking about it for a while, go back to your holiday rota problem and think about the two things in tandem – sugar and holiday rotas. See how thinking about sugar can help to stimulate ideas.

- Sugar makes you fat, so you need to exercise to lose weight. Maybe some of your employees might trade part of their holiday entitlement for membership of a good local gym. That would ease the pressure. Or maybe everyone would co-operate better if the company offered a free weekend at a health farm for the whole team in exchange for two days' fewer holiday each and an amicable settlement of dates.

- Sugar comes in lumps or grains – and holidays come in weeks or days. Perhaps people who take no more than four days' holiday at a time could be given an extra two days a year. Or those who avoid July and August could earn an extra entitlement.

- Thinking about sugar being sweet might make you think of sweeteners. How can you tempt people to give up their favourite holiday dates? Could you lay on some exciting event in the middle of the coveted holiday period to persuade people to stay? A meal at the best restaurant in town? A team weekend away?

Don't worry about whether you have the authority to implement these ideas. Once you've decided which are workable, you can present them to whoever does have the authority. If they are effective, you'll still get at least some of the credit – all if you're lucky. If the person you bring the idea to is the one who decides whether you get what you want at work, it doesn't matter if no one else knows it was your idea so long as they do.

Drawing techniques

The creative function is located in the right side of the brain, along with visual perception, while verbal skills are handled in the left brain. So if you use visual rather than verbal techniques, they can connect with your creative powers more readily since they are closer together. This is why many people find that doodling and drawing are more creative than verbal techniques.

Many people find that doodling and drawing are more creative than verbal techniques.

One of the simplest methods is simply to draw the challenge as you see it. To deal with the oversubscribed holiday period problem, for example, you might decide to draw lots of aeroplanes all over the page, or a long line of suitcases. Maybe you would draw an empty office building, or a ridiculously crowded palm-fringed beach. We're all different, and the idea is simply to draw whatever comes into your head. You're exercising the creative side of your brain to doodle or draw, and you are focusing on the problem or challenge at the same time. The result is very often that you stimulate an idea which leads you to a new and creative solution.

Doodles are more abstract than drawings, and some people find this free-form approach more stimulating. The idea is to concentrate on your challenge while you just doodle at random. When you've filled the page, look at what you've drawn and you should see shapes or patterns which give you a new perspective on the question.

Wacky doodles

If you find doodling effective and you want to vary the doodles you do to bring a more creative, unconscious energy to bear, try something like:

- finger painting doodles or using an airbrush
- doodling with your eyes closed
- doodling with the hand you don't normally use.

Keep out of the rut

You should find that these techniques are a big help when it comes to being more creative. However, if you keep using the same techniques over and over, your mind will simply create a new rut to get stuck in. It's essential to break with habitual patterns by varying the techniques you use.

It's essential to break with habitual patterns by varying the techniques you use.

There are plenty of books on business creativity; if you want to discover more techniques you can easily find them. You'll also find techniques for being creative in a group – especially valuable if you're a manager. If you can earn a reputation for leading a creative team, that will give you even more clout when it comes to getting those extra rewards.

Summary

In order to be creative, you need to train your mind to think in new, more creative patterns. Learn a few basic creativity techniques and apply them to any question or challenge which you feel calls for a creative solution. And remember that the more ideas you generate in total, the more good ideas there will be among them.

CHAPTER TWELVE

Be persuasive

Deep down, most of us are like children, only bigger. You know that if you want a child to do something they've never done before, they're far more likely to agree to it if you tell them that it will be exciting and fun than if you tell them to do it 'because I say so'. Customers, colleagues and bosses are much the same – we all are. And the same techniques tend to be just as effective on grown-ups. It's absolutely vital to learn to use these techniques if you're going to get what you want.

> **Deep down, most of us are like children, only bigger.**

There are two key stages in persuading people round to your way of thinking.

1 Show you're on their side.

2 Lead them over to your side.

The psychology of persuasion

The process of debating an argument, or reading a proposal, is more emotional (albeit unconsciously) than you might think. The person you're talking to needs to feel that you understand their position. In a sense, it shows that you accept them, it puts you both on the same team. This feeling of acceptance is surprisingly important, even to the most hard-bitten business people. So you've got to show that you're starting in the other person's camp, even if you disagree with their current point of view.

In other words, you have to start by convincing them that you're on their side. Show that you can see why your colleague resents a change in the system, or why your boss is reluctant to give you more responsibility, or why your customer feels your product is overpriced. Anything else would antagonize them, obviously, because the implication would be that their judgement was not as good as yours. And nobody wants to hear that.

Natural empathy

When you say to a child, 'because I say so', you're telling them that you know more than them, and that your opinion is more important than theirs. No wonder they get annoyed. But when you say to them, 'Go on – it'll be fun and exciting', you're saying that you understand what they want, and their judgement is valid – it's OK to want to do fun, exciting things. You're on their side. It's hardly surprising that adopting a sympathetic attitude earns you a sympathetic response.

Once you're metaphorically standing alongside the other person – they've accepted you and they're confident that you've accepted them – you can gently start to lead them where you want them to go. You can explain things from their perspective and guide them towards the right decision. They're much more likely to listen to you when you're standing next to them. If you were miles away shouting, 'Come over here – it's much nicer, honest!,' they could reasonably ask 'How do you know? You don't know what it's like over here'.

So that's the key to the psychology. Don't stand in your entrenched position shouting 'Come here!' If you want them to agree to your proposal, you have to do the work. Go over to them, take their hand and lead them back to your position.

All the techniques in this chapter are ways of convincing the other person that you're on their side, or guiding them back to your side without losing them en route. They are techniques that work in meetings, in one-to-one discussions, at presentations, in letters and when you write a proposal to persuade your boss or customer to accept an idea.

Show you're on their side

Here are the key techniques you need to use to clinch the first half of the persuading process: showing you're on their side. Even if the other person doesn't need a lot of convincing, you still need to use these techniques to be sure you don't alienate or antagonize them.

Express yourself from the other person's point of view

Imagine you're on the receiving end. It's much harder to bring yourself to agree with someone who clearly doesn't see things your way – who wants to satisfy their own needs and not yours. I once had a phone call from an estate agent who said, 'I've got your name on our mailing list – are you still looking for a house?' I replied, 'I don't think so. I've seen a house through another agent that looks just right and I've put in an offer.' The estate agent replied, 'Oh no. What a shame!'

She then went on to ask me to let her know if it fell through. I no longer felt, however, that she actually wanted the same thing as me at all. I wanted to find a house that met my needs. She wanted me to find a house which gave her a commission.

Actually, if we think about it we know perfectly well that's what all estate agents want. But we never usually consider it – we let ourselves believe that the estate agent just wants us to be happy. If you're an estate agent, you don't actually have the huge task of convincing your customer that you're more interested in their happiness than your own wages. All you have to do is to show that you're looking at it from their point of view. Just say, 'Congratulations – I hope it works out.' It makes them feel that you understand and you accept their position.

It's important to put yourself in the other person's position from the very beginning. If you're adopting a formal process of persuasion, such as writing a proposal, a letter or a presentation, start by stating the other person's point of view. And make sure that you accept it as being valid; never give the impression (even if it's the truth) that you don't see their problem as a problem at all.

It's important to put yourself in the other person's position from the very beginning.

Massage their ego

Everyone has an ego, whether it shows or not. They want to know that they're important, and one way to do this is to show that their point of view is important. If you can do this, you'll encourage them to listen to you in turn.

Suppose the board has asked you to write a proposal. Let's say they're not happy with the number of staff in your department, and would like you to review the possibility of reducing your staffing level. You, on the other hand, feel your staff are already overstretched and it would be outrageous to lay any of them off and put the rest under even more pressure.

You should still explain the problem as they see it. Once you do that, they'll feel you're on their side, so they're far more likely to believe you when you explain later on that, unfortunately, any change in the arrangements would lead to more problems than it would solve.

Show you understand the real issues

No one is going to take your advice if they think you don't understand what's going on. So make sure you not only find out what the key factors are for the other person, but actively demonstrate that you understand.

So if you're trying to persuade a tricky colleague that your proposed new system will make their life easier, find out why they're resisting it. Then you can show you understand by explaining that you recognize the proposed changes will mean that their paperwork doesn't get signed off until later in the day, and that if more than one of their team is off sick, the backlog could pile up quickly. This should make your colleague realize that you really have concerned yourself with the issues that matter to them, as well as the ones that directly affect you.

No one is going to take your advice if they think you don't understand what's going on.

Sometimes you can find out very easily what the real issues are for the other person. It can be harder when you're dealing with major issues and are writing a proposal or giving a presentation to try to get the decision you want. To get to the root of these issues from the other person's perspective you could try some of the following suggestions.

- Ask them – just because you don't know about a certain factor, it doesn't automatically mean you're not supposed to. If you ask, 'Is there anything I might not know about which is relevant?', they could well say, 'You've heard about the launch being brought forward, have you?'

- Read minutes of relevant recent meetings if you can.

- Talk to your colleagues and your boss.

- Talk to *their* colleagues.

- Talk to key people in other relevant departments or organizations. Personnel may know better than you what's being planned for other departments' staffing levels, or a supplier might know more than you about one of your customers.

- Look through back issues of relevant trade journals.

Get the lowdown

If you're trying to persuade a customer to buy your product or accept a particular deal, you may have to work a little harder to find out what they see as the real issues. You can ask them, and also read their newsletters or annual reports. Look at trade publications for their industry. If you have good contacts elsewhere in their organization, talk to them.

Be objective

Your own credibility is vital. No one is going to allow you to lead them round to your way of thinking if they don't trust your judgement. So you need to make it very clear that you are judging the facts objectively. If the data suggested a different route, you would take it; you're only recom-

No one is going to allow you to lead them round to your way of thinking if they don't trust your judgement.

mending this particular idea or decision because you genuinely consider that it is best for everyone: that's the feeling you want the other person to come away with. It's usually true, in fact. If you don't think you're recommending the best option, why are you doing it? There are two important ways to make sure you appear objective:

1 Don't use subjective judgements.

2 Prefer hard facts to unsupported assertions.

Don't use subjective judgements

Avoid subjective words like 'best' – choose an objective alternative. Say it's the 'fastest' or the 'most accurate'; these are statements you can prove. Keep away from fancy adjectives – 'its incredible speed' or 'stunning performance'. It's far more persuasive to specify: 'speeds up to 120 mph' or 'performance which, in tests, cut down administrative time by 45 per cent'.

If you can use objective measures you will carry far more clout. It doesn't sound as if you have a vested interest; you're simply stating the facts. If you have no objective measure, don't use subjective statements as an alternative – if you're asked to justify them you'll be in trouble.

Prefer hard facts to unsupported assertions

If you want to say that your idea is the most exciting, the cheapest or the most productive, *always* back it up. Equally, if you want to suggest that any other option is less reliable, needs more maintenance or is slower to operate, use supporting data to justify your argument.

If you can't find – or commission – the data you need, don't include the fact.

If you can't find – or commission – the data you need, don't include the fact.

If you *can't* back it up, it really isn't a fact anyway, it's an opinion or a supposition. There are degrees of certainty in this kind of information, of course. You might be able to say anything from, 'seven independent tests, four of them conducted live on prime time television, showed conclusively that . . .', to 'initial tests haven't been completed yet, but the early findings indicate that . . .' The more conclusive, the better. But anything legitimate is better than nothing.

And if you can't justify it . . .

Make sure that you never make any assertions which you can't justify. In a written proposal you might decide to put the supporting information in an appendix, or you might even choose not to include it in the final document at all. If you're giving a presentation you may simply include it in your handout material, or wait and see if anyone asks. But if you're asked for evidence to back up your claim, you must be able to produce it.

Lead them over to your side

So now, after showing you're on their side, you're standing shoulder to shoulder with the other person. They know you under-stand their situation and their needs. You have shown them your judgement is sound and your information accurate. Now it's time to lead them back over to your side. But do it as if you were treading on eggshells.

> **Make sure that you never make any assertions which you can't justify.**

Be fair

Treat all the opposing arguments fairly. If one of the other options works out cheaper than the one you're proposing, don't attempt to hide the fact. It's not worth the risk of getting found out – which you almost certainly will be. If the other person spots you omitting important data, or trying to mis-lead them, not only have you lost your credibility for now, but for evermore. Even if they don't spot it now, they may do after they've made the decision and started to use your new system, or given you the extra staff you wanted, or started using the product you've sold them.

A false statement or the suppression of a relevant fact is like the thirteenth chime of a clock: it isn't just obviously wrong in itself; it also casts doubt on the previous twelve.

Furthermore, if this is a proposal to a customer and you make a derogatory comment about one of your competitors, the customer is unlikely to believe you anyway. Their response will simply be, 'Well they would say that, wouldn't they?' And if they already use your competitor's product, they will feel you are insulting their judgement. The same applies if you are trying to persuade your boss to promote your idea and you cast aspersions on your colleague's competing idea.

If, on the other hand, they see you being scrupulously fair, they will have far more faith in your judgement, and be happy to follow you to whatever conclusion you decide to lead them.

Just because you're being fair, however, you don't have to draw attention to any weak points in your own argument.

Just because you're being fair, however, you don't have to draw attention to any weak points in your own argument. All the facts should be there, but you can choose how to present them. Suppose you're in a meeting, talking about cost comparisons between all the possible options, and your preference happens to be the most expensive. You can't lie, and you can't very well omit to discuss the cost, but you can at least make sure that you don't mention the price immediately next to the cheapest option. There's no point drawing attention to it.

Don't pooh-pooh the other possibilities

Your listener or reader may consider all the possibilities to be viable options. That's why you're discussing them. If someone wants to soft boil an egg for their breakfast and is deciding how long to cook it for, you might suggest three minutes, four minutes or five. But you're not going to bother suggesting they get up at 5 o'clock in the morning, coat the egg in wax and leave it in the sun for three hours while they go back to bed. You know that option isn't in the running.

Never forget that the other person is giving serious consideration to all the other possibilities under discussion. So if you criticize any of the options, however subtly, you are, in effect, insulting their judgement. That doesn't mean you have to flatter the alternatives to your idea – simply remain objective about them. This helps to convince the other person that you're on their side – like them, you too are considering the alternatives.

Give them an excuse to change their minds

Suppose you're putting a proposal to the whole board, half a dozen or more people. Some of them may already have expressed strong views on the subject of your proposal. You know what people are like (we're back to the psychology again) – they don't like backing down. So give them an excuse. Explain that high staffing levels are indeed usually an unnecessary expense; you'd be the first to agree. But in fact this instance is different. You need two extra experienced staff to work on the new software, which will free up four people to sell full time, so the increased staffing level will pay for itself in the first three months.

You've now given the board members an excuse to come round to your view without losing face. They can say, 'You see, I was right. Increasing staff isn't cost effective as a rule. But of course, if they're experienced in the new technology, that could make a difference . . .'

Lots of faces to save

If you have several people to persuade, say at a meeting, they may each have opposing views. If this is so, you'll need to be very diplomatic to make sure that they don't lose face in relation to each other, as well as to you.

State your preferred option last

Your approach to the possibilities you've laid out may vary. For a sales proposal it may well be that the only option you'll be happy with is the one you're recommending – or you may hope that if they don't buy your top-of-the-range vans they will buy the middle-range ones, rather than going to another supplier. If you're presenting an internal proposal to a meeting, you might have a first choice, but also several other options you consider to be perfectly acceptable. So don't back yourself into a corner by making one

Whether you're pointing up your number one choice subtly or obviously, put it last.

clear recommendation if there are others which you would settle for. But whether you're pointing up your number one choice subtly or obviously, put it last. That way it's freshest in the other people's minds when they start to think about your recommendations.

Anticipate objections

If you're in a meeting, or giving a presentation, you can ask the person you're talking to whether they have any comments or questions. On paper you don't have that opportunity, so you have to work out in advance what comments or questions they might have to be sure you deal with them. (In fact, face to face or on paper, you should still anticipate objections so that you have a ready answer. The difference is simply that in a letter or a written proposal, you need to include the answers to those objections.)

If you think the reader might think the cost of your proposal is too high, for example, you'll need to include data showing how over time it works out as more cost effective, or how much more they're getting for their money. If they're likely to think that your idea will be too disruptive, indicate how easy it will be to operate once it's up and running. If they may worry that it needs more experienced staff to operate it, explain how quickly current staff can be trained to do it. And so on. Have these arguments ready if you're persuading people face to face; put them down in the proposal if you're persuading them on paper.

Summary

Once you've mastered these techniques, you'll have far greater success persuading people to give you what you want. The crux of it is to understand the psychology. And you do that by:

Showing them you're on their side:

- Express yourself from the other person's point of view.
- Show you understand the real issues.
- Be objective.

Leading them over to your side:

- Be fair.
- Don't pooh-pooh the other possibilities.
- Give the other person an excuse to change their mind.
- State your preferred option last.
- Anticipate objections.

CHAPTER THIRTEEN

Negotiate effectively

If what you want at work depends on someone else's co-operation – your boss, a colleague or another manager, a customer, a supplier – you won't generally get it unless you learn to negotiate. You need to bargain to get a promotion or pay rise, to find better working relationships with tricky people, to close a deal with a customer or supplier, to get your boss to give you more time off or a bigger expenses allowance or a smarter office. Once you've put in all the ground-work to ensure that you have a convincing case for get-ting what you want, this is how you finally clinch it.

> **If what you want at work depends on someone else's co-operation, you won't generally get it unless you learn to negotiate.**

It's extremely rare that when you ask for what you want, you're told, 'Yes, sure, here it is. Take it.' The person you're asking may see that you deserve it (or they may not), but there are other pressures on them. Your boss might want to give you a pay rise but be concerned that everyone else will ask for one too. Your customer might think your terms are perfectly fair, but their budget is too tight to accommodate them. Your colleague might understand exactly why you want a certain responsibility, but they don't want to suffer the loss of status they think will go with yielding the responsibility to you.

This is when the negotiating begins, and if the other person is a skilled negotiator you could find them running rings round you. You're in danger of finding you've agreed to something you're not in the least happy with, and you can't quite remember how you came to say yes to it.

But never fear. The really important rules of negotiating are few and simple, and you're just about to learn them. They will scupper any dirty tricks as well as any clean, honest techniques on the other person's part, and they

The really important rules of negotiating are few and simple. will give you every chance of coming out of the negotiating game on top. What's more, as we'll see in a moment, you can massage their ego at the same time, because the aim is for *both* of you to come out feeling like winners.

Win/win negotiating

The real aim of a negotiation is for both parties to arrive at a mutually satisfactory solution: both pulling together, on the same side, to find an outcome that works for everyone. But somehow that's not what it feels like. It *feels* as though you're lined up on opposite sides of a battleground, each doing your best to score points at the other's expense. In fact, only a mutually acceptable solution ever works. If the other person really isn't prepared to give you what you want, they won't. And if you're really not prepared to accept their best offer, you'll refuse it.

But although the results of negotiating depend on both sides working together as a team, the psychology of the process does have more to do with a battleground mentality. And neither side is going to give up the fight until they have won.

Watch that ego

The reason everyone wants to come out a winner is the simple matter of not losing face. Even if your boss can afford to give you a rise, they want to feel they've made you work for it. Even if your customer can see you're offering a fair deal, they want to know they've got the best they can for their company. The bigger their ego, the more resounding they will want to feel their success has been. So take this into account when you negotiate.

That may sound like a recipe for a very long and fruitless argument, but it doesn't have to be. Your meeting can be amicable and successful, and be concluded swiftly, on one condition: that you both emerge as the winner.

Sounds daft? It may sound it, but it is actually very smart. On a traditional battlefield you could tell who had won by how many people on each side were dead, and by who was left wearing the crown. In the modern battleground of negotiations, however, things aren't so straightforward. In fact, the only way you can tell if you've won is if you *feel* like a winner.

> **In the modern battleground of negotiations, the only way you can tell if you've won is if you *feel* like a winner.**

And that works to your advantage. Your task is to make sure that the other person feels they have won. If they feel like a winner, they are one – by any reasonable definition. So how do you make them feel like a winner without giving yourself the sensation of having lost? The answer is that you make concessions, you let them beat you down. However, as you'll see, you won't be making concessions without getting something in return. And the reason you can let them beat you down is because you start by asking for more than you expect to get.

You need to begin by making a justifiable request – but ask for the best you can defend. The best terms, the biggest pay rise, the maximum co-operation. That way, you can afford to be beaten down. Suppose you're asking the boss for a pay rise and you really feel you deserve a 7 per cent increase. But you could put forward a valid case for a 10 per cent rise. So your approach is simple: you ask for 10 per cent, and you allow yourself to be beaten down to seven. You've got what you wanted all along, and your boss feels they have knocked you down by 3 per cent – they feel like a winner too. That's win/win negotiating.

Know your bottom line

OK, that's the other person sorted out – they'll definitely end up feeling like a winner. But what about you? How far are you going to let them beat you down before you come out feeling like a loser? You have to go into this negotiation knowing what is the least you are prepared to settle for. Otherwise you may come out with nothing. It's no good saying 'We'll give you a 30 per cent discount', and then, when your customer declines, saying, 'Oh well, it was worth a try', and leaving.

It's up to you to decide what your bottom line is. Suppose you want to change your working hours. Maybe your family circumstances have changed and you need to be home by a certain time to look after the kids. Or perhaps you simply feel that you're being exploited and you don't want to work for an organization that doesn't appreciate and reward you. Maybe you won't be happy unless you're away from the office by 5pm every day, or perhaps you'd settle for an undertaking to cut down your hours gradually so long as you continue to meet your agreed performance target. Your bottom line may be well below the figure you're really aiming for, or it may be the same figure.

The important thing is to know your bottom line and then stick to it. And, of course, decide what you'll do if the other person refuses even that much (although if you're realistic, and you've done your homework, you should be asking for something you know the other person can afford to give you). If you're not ready to hold out for the bottom line figure, there's little point in negotiating. If you don't hold firm you might as well just say, 'How about it?' to your boss on the off chance they'll give you two afternoons off a week without argument.

The important thing is to know your bottom line and then stick to it.

Leverage? What leverage?

When you're negotiating for better pay or conditions with your boss, you might be thinking that you have nothing to negotiate with unless you're prepared to hand in your notice. If you're not, all your boss has to do is flatly refuse, and that's that. Not so. You're here because you are worth more than you're getting. That extra value is your leverage. Threats don't work, but you can always find other ways of phrasing the point you're making. For example, 'I feel I'm worth more than I'm earning because of all the extra hours I put in. If those extra hours weren't going to be rewarded, I would have to ask myself why I work them.' You're not threatening to work to rule, but your boss can see that you have bargaining counters too.

By the way, whatever you do, don't give away what your bottom line is. 'It's for you to know and them to find out', as they say. At least, let them think they've found out by beating you down to it. But if you're canny, they won't ever haggle you down that far. If the other person finds out what your bottom line is, they won't stop until they've ground you down to it. So don't let them find out until they reach it. At that point you can, if you wish, say, 'That's my absolute bottom line.'

And don't, whatever you do, cry wolf. If you insist you've reached your bottom line and then subsequently agree to drop below it, the other person will quite reasonably disbelieve you when you finally claim – truthfully – that yet another figure really *is* your bottom line. And if they don't believe you, they'll keep trying to batter you down and the pair of you may never reach an agreement that works.

Negotiating techniques

So you're ready to go. You're going to make the other person feel like a winner, and you're going to make sure you end up a winner too, by fixing a bottom line in your mind and sticking to it. So now it's time to look at the specific techniques of negotiating – all those tricks which will ensure that you arrive at a win/win solution.

Find all the variables

Suppose you can only give your customer a 30 per cent discount – that's your bottom line – and *they* know they need at least 32 per cent to meet their budget. It's pretty hard to see how you're going to find any common ground, even with the best will in the world. So what do you do? I can't really answer that, because you shouldn't really get into this position in the first place. The solution is to avoid this kind of stalemate altogether.

And the way you do that is by finding variables – other factors you can bring into the negotiation. For example:

- If your customer simply doesn't have the budget at the moment, you could suggest that if they can contract for a minimum size of order, you'll agree to stage payments set in a way they can afford.

- Maybe you can agree the discount they want now, if they'll contract for a minimum of three years.

- Perhaps you could agree a lower standard elsewhere to save the cost of the bigger discount – maybe slower delivery times, or they part assemble the goods.

All of these are good examples of the factors which can help to bring the two sides closer together in a negotiation. The more variables you have, the more room for manoeuvre there is in the overall negotiation. So think through all the possible variables you could introduce, both when you're preparing for the negotiation and during the course of it. Never stop looking for variables until you've reached an agreement you're both happy with.

The more variables you have, the more room for manoeuvre there is in the overall negotiation.

Get all the cards on the table

If the other person is a tricksy kind of negotiator, there's one ace they'll be holding up their sleeve. They may well have concessions they want from you before they will agree to what you want.

Say you're asking your boss for a promotion. They might want you to agree to delay the promotion, or to take on extra responsibilities beyond what you'd expect. And if they are an underhand dealer, they will wait until the last minute to spring this on you. In other words, they will wait until you've pretty well agreed on the terms of the promotion. And then out of the blue, 'Oh, and I'd like you to take over dealing with Philippa's accounts while she's on maternity leave.' Now, it's not that you necessarily don't want to take over Philippa's accounts. It's just that if you do, that will increase your value even more, and with it the size of pay rise that goes with the promotion. But hang on, you'd almost finished negotiating, and your boss knows that you were about to accept a 3 per cent rise. It's much harder now for you to backtrack and insist that you won't take less than 4 per cent. And your boss knows it.

The way to prevent this is very simple: ask the other person to put all their cards on the table, and do the same thing yourself. That way, you can balance all the issues against each other. All you have to do is to say, for example, 'I want to talk to you about promotion, and I'd also like to discuss my responsibilities. Are there any other issues we need to discuss at the same time?' You've made it extremely difficult for your boss to keep back the fact that they want to talk to you about covering for Philippa while she's away. If they don't mention it, and then spring it on you later, you have the moral high ground and will find it much easier to insist that it be excluded from the discussion, or that you go back over the other points you've agreed and revise them in the light of the new information.

Never give free concessions

This is a simple but critical rule for negotiating. All it means is that if the other person asks you to reduce your request, you don't simply say yes; you trade the concession for a matching concession on their part.

- If your difficult colleague says, 'I can give you the data you need, but not until the end of each month', you don't simply say, 'OK, then'. You say, 'So long as it's presented in the final format and not simply in draft'.

- When your boss says, 'You can't have a pay rise, but I can give you a commission bonus', you say, 'If we do it that way, the commission would need to be at least 5 per cent of gross'.

- When a customer says, 'I need at least 32 per cent', you say, 'I need a guarantee that you'll order a minimum of 5,000 a month, in that case'.

You've got the idea. This principle is crucial simply because it means that you end up with a better deal. Every time you lose something, you also gain something. Just make sure the concessions you gain roughly match the value of those you are giving.

Tough cookie

When you don't give free concessions, the other person will soon learn that you are a tough negotiator. They'll think twice about asking concessions from you when they realize that every time they do, they have to give up something themselves. And in the long term, too, it's a good thing if regular colleagues, managers and customers know you are no pushover when it comes to negotiating.

Agree to all or nothing

The way you reach a final settlement in your negotiation is by moving all the variables around until they balance. So, for example, if your salary is going up by less than you wanted, you won't agree to defer it by much. Of course you could defer it by more, but then you'd want a larger or smaller proportion of it to be performance-related. Or maybe you're happy to agree to a larger proportion being performance-linked, but only so long as the return on good performance is higher. It's as though all these factors are on sliding scales, and you are sliding one up as another goes down, keeping them all in a balance to produce a settlement you're happy with.

The one thing you mustn't do is to agree to any one variable before you agree to the rest of them. It would mean one of your sliders was stuck fast, and you couldn't adjust it to bring the whole thing into balance. This makes it far harder to agree on a final deal, and you may have to give more ground than you wanted on one of your other sliding scales to get a balance.

So you want to outlaw from the negotiation any comment such as, 'Right, we've agreed the discount. Now let's talk about how big the order will be.' Don't agree any such thing, and if the other person tries to railroad you with a comment like this, just say, 'We haven't finalized the discount yet; I'm still considering it. But I'm happy to go on and discuss the order.'

Rounding off

Once it is clear that you have found a balance that you are both happy with, that's the time to sum up, outlining all the key points clearly: 'So we're agreed then. You'll give me all the data in final form at the end of each month. If there's going to be a problem, you'll let me know by the 20th of the month. And I can get the re-order sheets back to you in time for the 10th.' The simplest thing now is to agree with the other person which one of the two of you should record the outcome of the meeting in writing, just so you can be sure that it gets put down in black and white, for future reference.

The way to negotiate is to make sure that both you and the other person come out of the meeting feeling that you've won.

Don't be surprised if your boss or your customer doesn't give you a conclusive 'yes' or 'no' on the spot. Even if they negotiate the best deal they think they can get, they may still need to get their decision approved by senior management before they can go ahead. If you've given them the salient facts and argued your case well, you should have set them up nicely to argue your position on your behalf. If they tell you they have to refer the decision upwards, ask if you can supply any other information to help them.

Summary

The way to negotiate is to make sure that both you and the other person come out of the meeting feeling that you've won. If you start by asking for a justifiable deal but one which is higher than you are happy to settle for, you can allow yourself to be beaten down. One of the components of this on your part is to know exactly what your bottom line is so you can be certain you don't agree to a deal which falls below it. The key techniques for achieving this kind of win/win outcome are:

- Find all the variables.
- Get all the cards on the table.
- Never give free concessions.
- Agree to all or nothing.

More power to your
[business-mind]

Even at the end there's more we can learn. More that *we* can learn from your experience of this book, and more ways to add to *your* learning experience.

For who to read, what to know and where to go in the world of business, visit us at **business-minds.com**.

Here you can find out more about the people and ideas that can make you and your business more innovative and productive. Each month our e-newsletter, *Business-minds Express*, delivers an infusion of thought leadership, guru interviews, new business practice and reviews of key business resources directly to you. Subscribe for free at

▶ **www.business-minds.com/goto/newsletters**

Here you can also connect with ways of putting these ideas to work. Spreading knowledge is a great way to improve performance and enhance business relationships. If you found this book useful, then so might your colleagues or customers. If you would like to explore corporate purchases or custom editions personalised with your brand or message, then just get in touch at

▶ **www.business-minds.com/corporatesales**

We're also keen to learn from your experience of our business books – so tell us what you think of this book and what's on *your* business mind with an online reader report at business-minds.com. Together with our authors, we'd like to hear more from you and explore new ways to help make these ideas work at

▶ **www.business-minds.com/goto/feedback**

[www.business-minds.com
www.financialminds.com]